JN102229

The kingen Minimal English Test

音声
CD付

牧 秀樹

金言版

最小英語テスト （kMET） ドリル

金言版

開拓社

まえがき

「世界の偉人の言葉，英語で言ったら受けるかも。」そんな思いで，このドリルを作りました。英語を勉強の一つだと考えたら，途端にやる気がなくなるかもしれませんが，気の利いた先人の言葉を，ちらっと英語で言ってみたら，会話が妙に弾むかもしれません。もう英語なんて，笑いを取る手段ですよ。

CD を使って，1 回 5 分程度で終わる問題が，14 題収載されています。このドリルにある簡易テストは，最小英語テスト金言版 (The kingen Minimal English Test = kMET) と呼びます。kMET の基本的な考え方は，もともとは，拙著『The Minimal English Test (最小英語テスト) 研究』(2018) で提唱された最小英語テスト (The Minimal English Test =MET) から来ています。

私が岐阜大学地域科学部で過去 17 年間調査した結果，MET には，二つの機能があることが分かってきました。一つは，MET には，英語能力を測定する機能があること。MET は，ちょうど，理科の実験に使用する**リトマス紙**に似ています。短時間で，学習者の英語能力をだいたい測定できるという点においてです。

もう一つは，MET には，英語能力を向上させる機能があること。MET は，ちょうど，陰山英男立命館小学校副校長・立命館大学教授の『**百ます計算**』や川島隆太東北大学加齢医学研究所教授の『**脳トレ**』に似ています。短時間の簡単な作業を繰り返し行うことで，脳が活性化し，一定の英語能力の向上が見られるという点においてです。

この kMET ドリルは，MET の二つ目の機能を使って，みなさんの英語の「**金言力**」を上げるお手伝いをしようと，作られました。高校の授業であれば，授業の最初の「帯」活動としても，有効に活用できると思います。

本ドリルの英語音声は，マイケル・ロプレスティ (Michael LoPresti) 氏による録音です。米国バージニア州出身の英語母語話者で，現在，東京大学薬学部医薬政策学講座に在籍し，薬学の博士号取得を目指しています。ウエスト・バージニア州のセイラム - テイキョウ大学日本研究学部で私と共に学び，その後，フロリダ州立大学で人口統計学と経済学で修士号を取得しました。マイケル・ロプレスティ氏とともに，私の研究室所属学生の姚夏蔭氏，呉文亮氏，靳暁雨氏にも，本ドリルの作成に惜しみなく尽力してくれたことに感謝します。また，困難な時世の中，本書の出版を引き受けてくださった開拓社の川田賢氏に感謝いたします。本書に現れる金言は，癒しツアー (2020) を部分的に参考にしています。日本語訳は，全て私によるものです。

最後に，本ドリルを作成しながら分かってきたことは，こんなことです。「金言には，難しい言葉がない。」金言か！

2020 年 6 月　　牧 秀樹

2

目　次

kMET のやり方

　kMET は，CD から流れてくる英文を聞きながら，単語を埋めるだけの簡単なテストです。CD だけを聞いていれば，それほど速いとは感じませんが，いったんテストが始まると，突然，襲い掛かるように速く感じます。ですから，単語が，聞きとれなかったり，書ききれなかったりした場合は，あきらめて，すぐに，次の空所に移るようにしてください。そうしないと，一度に5つくらい空所が吹っ飛んでしまうことがあり，得点の低下につながってしまいます。

　1題終わるごとに，次のページに日本語訳と解答があるので，答え合わせをしながら，書ききれなかった箇所を確認し，また，意味が分からなかった箇所も，同時に確認してください。日本語訳は，なるべく理解しやすいように，あえて，英文を前から訳しています。英語母語話者は，実際この順番で文の意味を理解していますので，わざわざ，英文で最初のほうに現れる動詞を，長い日本文の最後に置かないようにしています。

　では，いよいよ，次のページから，どうぞ，kMET で遊んでください。「世界の偉人の言葉，英語で言ったら受けるかも！」

kMET 問題

　本書には，問題が 14 題あります。各問題には，空所（　　　）があります。CD を聞きながら，（　　　）の中に，4 文字以下（最大で 4 文字）の英単語を入れて下さい。

　1 題終わるごとに，答え合わせをすることができます。各問題の次のページには，その英文の日本語訳が，そして，その次のページには，解答が太字で示されています。

　答え合わせが終わったら，問題のページに戻り，点数を記入しておくことができます。

1　科学者（1）

1-41 Albert Einstein／アルベルト・アインシュタイン（1879 年～1955 年）
42-45 Galileo Galilei／ガリレオ・ガリレイ（1564 年～1642 年）

CD を聞きながら，（　　　　　　　）の中に，4 文字以下の英単語を入れて下さい。

1. All religions, arts and sciences are branches of (　　　　　)[1] same tree.

2. Anyone who has never made (　　　　　)[2] mistake has never tried anything new.

3. Before God we are all equally (　　　　　)[3] and equally foolish.

4. Common sense is the collection of prejudices acquired by (　　　　　)[4] 18.

5. Everything should be made as simple as possible, but (　　　　　)[5] simpler.

6. Few are those who see with their (　　　　　)[6] eyes and feel with their own hearts.

7. Gravitation (　　　　　)[7] not be held responsible for people falling in (　　　　　)[8].

8. I believe that a simple and unassuming manner of (　　　　　)[9] is best for everyone, best both (　　　　　)[10] the body and the mind.

9. (　　　　　)[11] have no special talent.　I am only passionately curious.

10. (　　　　　)[12] never think of the future.　It comes soon enough.

11. If (　　　　　)[13] can't explain it to a six year old, (　　　　　)[14] don't understand it yourself.

12. Imagination is more important than knowledge.　Knowledge is limited.　Imagination encircles (　　　　　)[15] world.

13. In the middle of difficulty lies opportunity.

14. Information is (　　　　　　)^{16} knowledge.

15. Insanity: doing the same thing over and over again (　　　　　　)^{17} expecting different results.

16. Intellectuals solve problems, geniuses prevent them.

17. It is a miracle that curiosity survives formal education.

18. (　　　　　　)^{18} is high time that the ideal (　　　　　　)^{19} success should be replaced by the ideal of service.

19. It's not (　　　　　　)^{20} I'm so smart, it's just that I stay (　　　　　　)^{21} problems longer.

20. Learn from yesterday, live for today, hope for tomorrow. (　　　　　　)^{22} important thing is not to stop questioning.

21. Life (　　　　　　)^{23} like riding a bicycle. To keep your balance (　　　　　　)^{24} must keep moving.

22. Life isn't worth living, unless it is lived (　　　　　　)^{25} someone else.

23. Love is a better teacher than (　　　　　　)^{26}.

24. Men marry women with the hope they (　　　　　　)^{27} never change. Women marry men with the hope they (　　　　　　)^{28} change. Invariably they are both disappointed.

1 科学者 (1)

25. Most people say (　　　　　)²⁹ it is the intellect which makes a great scientist.

They (　　　　　)³⁰ wrong: it is character.

26. Never do anything against conscience even if (　　　　　)³¹ state demands it.

27. Only two things are infinite, the universe and human stupidity (　　　　　)³² I'm

not sure about the former.

28. Reading, after a certain age, diverts (　　　　　)³³ mind too much from its

creative pursuits. Any (　　　　　)³⁴ who reads too much and uses

(　　　　　)³⁵ own brain too little falls into lazy habits of thinking.

29. Science (　　　　　)³⁶ a wonderful thing if one does not have (　　　　　)³⁷

earn one's living at it.

30. Science without religion is lame, religion without science (　　　　　)³⁸ blind.

31. The difference between genius and stupidity is that genius has (　　　　　)³⁹

limits.

32. The more I learn, the more (　　　　　)⁴⁰ realize I don't know. The more I

realize (　　　　　)⁴¹ don't know, the more I want (　　　　　)⁴² learn.

33. The most incomprehensible thing about the universe is that (　　　　　)⁴³ is

comprehensible.

34. The only thing that interferes with (　　　　　)⁴⁴ learning is my education.

35. The value of a (　　　　　)⁴⁵ should be seen in what he gives (　　　　　)⁴⁶

not in what he is (　　　　　)⁴⁷ to receive.

36. The world is a dangerous place, not because (　　　　　)^{48} those who do evil, but because of those (　　　　　)^{49} look on and do nothing.

37. There are (　　　　　)^{50} two ways to live your life.　One (　　　　　)^{51} as though nothing is a miracle.　The other is (　　　　　)^{52} though everything is a miracle.

38. Truth is what stands the (　　　　　)^{53} of experience.

39. Try not to become a (　　　　　)^{54} of success but rather to become a man (　　　　　)^{55} value.

40. We cannot despair of humanity, since we ourselves are human beings.

41. When (　　　　　)^{56} man sits with a pretty girl (　　　　　)^{57} an hour, it seems like a minute.　(　　　　　)^{58} let him sit on a (　　　　　)^{59} stove for a minute —and it's longer than any (　　　　　)^{60}.　That's relativity.

42. All truths are easy to understand once (　　　　　)^{61} are discovered; the point is to discover them.

43. (　　　　　)^{62} yet, it moves.

44. Doubt is the father of invention.

45. (　　　　　)^{63} have never met a man so ignorant (　　　　　)^{64} I couldn't learn something from him.

1 科学者（1）日本語訳

問題英文の日本語訳を確認しよう。

1. すべての宗教，芸術，科学は，同じ一つの木の枝々だ。

2. 失敗した事がなければ，何も新しい事に挑戦しなかったのと同じだ。

3. 神の前において，人は平等に賢く，平等に愚かだ。

4. 常識とは，18歳までに獲得した偏見の集まりだ。

5. 何でもできる限りシンプルにすべきだ。しかし，シンプルすぎてはいけない。

6. 自分自身の目で見，自分自身の心で感じる人は，ほとんどいない。

7. 万有引力には，責任はない。人が恋に落ちるのに。

8. 私は，こう思う。シンプルで控えめな生き方が，誰にとっても，最も良いと。体にも，心にも。

9. 私に，特別な才能があるわけではない。ただ，人よりも好奇心が強いだけだ。

10. 私は，将来のことなど考えたことがない。すぐに来てしまうのだから。

11. それを6歳の子供に説明できなければ，あなたがそれを本当に理解しているとは言えない。

12. 想像力は知識より重要だ。知識には限界がある。想像力は世界を包み込む。

13. ピンチの中に，チャンスがある。

14. 情報は知識ではない。

15. 狂気とは，同じことを繰り返しながら，違う結果を望むことだ。

16. 知識人は問題を解決し，天才は問題を未然に防ぐ。

17. 正規の教育を受けて好奇心を失わなければ，奇跡だ。

18. もはやこんな時代が来ている。成功という理想が，奉仕という理想に取って替わられるべき時代が。

19. 私が特別賢いわけではない。ただ，人よりも，長く問題に関わっているだけだ。

20. 過去から学び，今日のために生き，未来に希望を抱け。大切なことは，問うことをやめてしまわないことだ。

21. 人生とは自転車に乗るようなものだ。倒れないようにするには走り続けなければならない。

22. 人生には価値がない。誰か他の人の為に生きていないのなら。

23. 愛は，義務より優れた教師だ。

24. 男が結婚する際，女が変わらないことを望む。女が結婚する際，男が変わることを望む。互いに失望しないはずはない。

25. 人は言う。偉大な科学者を生み出すのは知性だと。そうではない。それは，人格だ。

26. 良心に反することは，決してしてはならない。たとえ国家が要求しても。

27. 無限なものは二つある。それは，宇宙と人間の愚かさだ。ただ，前者については断言できないが。

28. 一定の年齢を過ぎたら，読書によって，独創的な探求ができなくなる。本を読みすぎて，自分自身の脳を使わなくなれば，考えない人間になってしまうからだ。

29. 科学は，素晴らしいものだ。生活の糧をそれから得るのでなければ。

30. 科学は宗教を持たなければ不完全で，宗教は科学を持たなければ盲目だ。

31. 天才と愚者との違いは，天才には限度があるということだ。

32. 学べば学ぶほど，自分がどれほど無知であるか分かる。自分の無知が分かれば分かるほど，一層学びたくなる。

33. 宇宙について最も理解しがたいことは，それが理解可能だということだ。

34. 私の学習を妨げた唯一のものは，私が受けた教育だ。

35. 人の価値は，その人が得るものではなく，その人が与えるもので分かる。

36. この世は危険な場所だ。それは，悪事を働く者がいるからではなく，それを見て，何もしない者がいるからだ。

37. 人生には，二つの道しかない。一つは，奇跡などまったく存在しないかのように生きること。もう一つは，すべてが奇跡であるかのように生きることだ。

38. 真理とは，経験という試練に耐え得るもののことだ。

39. 成功者になろうとせず，価値のある人間になろうとせよ。

40. 人間性について絶望してはいけない。なぜなら，我々は人間なのだから。

41. 可愛い女の子と一時間一緒にいると，一分しか経っていないように思える。しかし，熱いストーブの上に一分座らせられたら，どの一時間よりも長く感じられる。これが，相対性だ。

42. あらゆる真理は，容易に理解できる。一度発見されてしまえば。ただし，重要なのは，真理を発見することだ。

43. それでも地球は動いている。

44. 懐疑は発明の父だ。

45. 私は，こんな人に会ったことがない。愚かすぎて，何も学ぶべきものがない人に。

1 科学者（1）解答

1. All religions, arts and sciences are branches of (**the**)[1] same tree.

2. Anyone who has never made (**a**)[2] mistake has never tried anything new.

3. Before God we are all equally (**wise**)[3] and equally foolish.

4. Common sense is the collection of prejudices acquired by (**age**)[4] 18.

5. Everything should be made as simple as possible, but (**not**)[5] simpler.

6. Few are those who see with their (**own**)[6] eyes and feel with their own hearts.

7. Gravitation (**can**)[7] not be held responsible for people falling in (**love**)[8].

8. I believe that a simple and unassuming manner of (**life**)[9] is best for everyone, best both (**for**)[10] the body and the mind.

9. (**I**)[11] have no special talent. I am only passionately curious.

10. (**I**)[12] never think of the future. It comes soon enough.

11. If (**you**)[13] can't explain it to a six year old, (**you**)[14] don't understand it yourself.

12. Imagination is more important than knowledge. Knowledge is limited. Imagination encircles (**the**)[15] world.

13. In the middle of difficulty lies opportunity.

14. Information is (**not**)[16] knowledge.

15. Insanity: doing the same thing over and over again (**and**)[17] expecting different results.

16. Intellectuals solve problems, geniuses prevent them.

17. It is a miracle that curiosity survives formal education.

18. (**It**)[18] is high time that the ideal (**of**)[19] success should be replaced by the ideal of service.

19. It's not (**that**)[20] I'm so smart, it's just that I stay (**with**)[21] problems longer.

20. Learn from yesterday, live for today, hope for tomorrow. (**The**)[22] important thing is not to stop questioning.

21. Life (**is**)[23] like riding a bicycle. To keep your balance (**you**)[24] must keep moving.

22. Life isn't worth living, unless it is lived (**for**)[25] someone else.

23. Love is a better teacher than (**duty**)[26].

24. Men marry women with the hope they (**will**)[27] never change. Women marry men with the hope they (**will**)[28] change. Invariably they are both disappointed.

25. Most people say (**that**)[29] it is the intellect which makes a great scientist. They (**are**)[30] wrong: it is character.

26. Never do anything against conscience even if (**the**)[31] state demands it.

27. Only two things are infinite, the universe and human stupidity（**and**）^{32} I'm not sure about the former.

28. Reading, after a certain age, diverts（**the**）^{33} mind too much from its creative pursuits. Any（**man**）^{34} who reads too much and uses（**his**）^{35} own brain too little falls into lazy habits of thinking.

29. Science（**is**）^{36} a wonderful thing if one does not have（**to**）^{37} earn one's living at it.

30. Science without religion is lame, religion without science（**is**）^{38} blind.

31. The difference between genius and stupidity is that genius has（**its**）^{39} limits.

32. The more I learn, the more（**I**）^{40} realize I don't know. The more I realize（**I**）^{41} don't know, the more I want（**to**）^{42} learn.

33. The most incomprehensible thing about the universe is that（**it**）^{43} is comprehensible.

34. The only thing that interferes with（**my**）^{44} learning is my education.

35. The value of a（**man**）^{45} should be seen in what he gives（**and**）^{46} not in what he is（**able**）^{47} to receive.

36. The world is a dangerous place, not because（**of**）^{48} those who do evil, but because of those（**who**）^{49} look on and do nothing.

37. There are（**only**）^{50} two ways to live your life. One（**is**）^{51} as though nothing is a miracle. The other is（**as**）^{52} though everything is a miracle.

38. Truth is what stands the（**test**）^{53} of experience.

39. Try not to become a（**man**）^{54} of success but rather to become a man（**of**）^{55} value.

40. We cannot despair of humanity, since we ourselves are human beings.

41. When（**a**）^{56} man sits with a pretty girl（**for**）^{57} an hour, it seems like a minute. （**But**）^{58} let him sit on a（**hot**）^{59} stove for a minute—and it's longer than any（**hour**）^{60}. That's relativity.

42. All truths are easy to understand once（**they**）^{61} are discovered; the point is to discover them.

43. （**And**）^{62} yet, it moves.

44. Doubt is the father of invention.

45. （**I**）^{63} have never met a man so ignorant（**that**）^{64} I couldn't learn something from him.

2　哲学者 (1)

1-21 Socrates/ソクラテス (紀元前 469 年〜前 399 年)
22-35 Plato/プラトン (紀元前 427 年〜前 347 年)
36-45 Aristotle/アリストテレス (紀元前 384 年〜前 322 年)

CD を聞きながら，(　　　　　　　) の中に，4 文字以下の英単語を入れて下さい。

1. By all means marry; if you get (　　　　　)[1] good wife, you'll be happy.　If you (　　　　　)[2] a bad one, you'll become a philosopher.

2. Death may be (　　　　　)[3] greatest of all human blessings.

3. Do not do (　　　　　)[4] others what angers you if done to (　　　　　)[5] by others.

4. Employ your time in improving yourself by other men's writings, (　　　　　)[6] that you shall gain easily what others have labored (　　　　　)[7] for.

5. Envy is the ulcer of (　　　　　)[8] soul.

6. Having the fewest wants, I am nearest to (　　　　　)[9] gods.

7. He is richest who is content with (　　　　　)[10] least, for content is the wealth of nature.

8. I (　　　　　)[11] not an Athenian or a Greek, but (　　　　　)[12] citizen of the world.

9. I know nothing except the (　　　　　)[13] of my ignorance.

10. If a man (　　　　　)[14] proud of his wealth, he should not be praised until (　　　　　)[15] is known how he employs it.

11. Let (　　　　　)[16] who would move the world, first move himself.

12. Remember that there (   )^{17} nothing stable in human affairs; therefore avoid undue elation in prosperity, or undue depression in adversity.

13. The (   )^{18} of departure has arrived, and we go (   )^{19} ways—I to die and (   )^{20} to live.   Which is the better, only God knows.

14. (   )^{21} only good is knowledge and the (   )^{22} evil is ignorance.

15. The only true wisdom (   )^{23} in knowing you know nothing.

16. The unexamined life (   )^{24} not worth living.

17. The way to gain (   )^{25} good reputation is to endeavor to be (   )^{26} you desire to appear.

18. Think not those faithful who praise all (   )^{27} words and actions; but those who kindly reprove your faults.

19. You should (   )^{28} to live; not live to (   )^{29}.

20. Wealth does not bring goodness, but goodness brings wealth and every other blessing, both (   )^{30} the individual and to the state.

21. When (   )^{31} debate is over, slander becomes the tool of (   )^{32} loser.

22. The first and best victory is to conquer (   )^{33}.

23. Nothing in the affairs of men is worthy (   )^{34} great anxiety.

24. Be kind, for everyone you meet (   )^{35} fighting a harder battle.

25. At the touch of love, everyone becomes (   )^{36} poet.

2 哲学者 (1)

26. The eyes are the windows (   )^{37} the soul.

27. There are three classes of men; lovers (   )^{38} wisdom, lovers of honor, and lovers of gain.

28. Wise (   )^{39} speak because they have something to say; Fools because they (   )^{40} to say something.

29. The madness of love (   )^{41} the greatest of heaven's blessings.

30. Do not train a child (   )^{42} learn by force or harshness; but direct them to (   )^{43} by what amuses their minds, so that you (   )^{44} be better able to discover with accuracy the peculiar (   )^{45} of the genius of each.

31. Science is nothing (   )^{46} perception.

32. The beginning is the most important part (   )^{47} the work.

33. Rhythm and harmony find their way (   )^{48} the inward places of the soul.

34. Music gives a (   )^{49} to the universe, wings to the mind, flight to (   )^{50} imagination and life to everything.

35. Only the (   )^{51} have seen the end of (   )^{52}.

36. A friend to all is a friend (   )^{53} none.

37. All men by nature desire knowledge.

38. Anyone can become angry — (　　　　　)⁵⁴ is easy. But to be angry

    (　　　　　)⁵⁵ the right person, to the right degree, at the right (　　　　　)⁵⁶,

    for the right purpose, and in the right (　　　　　)⁵⁷ — this is not easy.

39. Bashfulness is (　　　　　)⁵⁸ ornament to youth, but a reproach to old

    (　　　　　)⁵⁹.

40. Courage is the first of human qualities because it is (　　　　　)⁶⁰ quality which

    guarantees the others.

41. Dignity does not consist in possessing honors, but (　　　　　)⁶¹ deserving

    them.

42. Excellence is an art won (　　　　　)⁶² training and habituation. We do not act

    rightly because (　　　　　)⁶³ have virtue or excellence, but we rather have

    those because (　　　　　)⁶⁴ have acted rightly.

43. For one swallow does not make (　　　　　)⁶⁵ summer, nor does one day; and

    so (　　　　　)⁶⁶ one day, or a short time, does (　　　　　)⁶⁷ make a man

    blessed and happy.

44. For (　　　　　)⁶⁸ things we have to learn before we can (　　　　　)⁶⁹ them,

    we learn by doing them.

45. Friendship is (　　　　　)⁷⁰ single soul dwelling in two bodies.

2 哲学者（1）日本語訳

問題英文の日本語訳を確認しよう。

1. いいから結婚せよ。良妻を持てば幸せになれるし，悪妻を持てば哲学者になれる。

2. 死は，最高のものかもしれない。人間に与えられたすべての恵みの中で。

3. 他人にしてはいけない。他人からされたらいやなことを。

4. 人の本をよく読んで自分を成長させよ。本は著者が苦労して得たことを，たやすく得させてくれるから。

5. 妬みとは，魂の腐ったものだ。

6. 最小限の欲望しか持っていないから，私は，神々に最も近い。

7. 最小のことで満足できる人が，最も裕福だ。何故なら，満足とは，自然が与えてくれる富だからだ。

8. 私は，アテネ人でも，ギリシア人でもない。世界市民だ。

9. 私は，知っている。自分が何も知らないということだけを。（無知の知）

10. 自分の富を自慢している者がいても，褒めてはいけない。その富をどのように使うかがはっきりするまでは。

11. 世界を動かしたければ，まず自分自身を動かせ。

12. 人間に関わることに安定などない。したがって，繁栄していれば，過度の喜びを避け，逆境にあれば，過度の落ち込みを避けよ。

13. 出発の時が来た。そして，我々は，それぞれの道を行く。私は死に，あなたは生きる。どちらが良いのか。それは，神だけが知っている。

14. 唯一の善は知識であり，唯一の悪は無知だ。

15. 唯一の真の賢さは，このことを知ることにある。自分が何も知らないということを。

16. 吟味されない人生は，過ごすに値しない。

17. 良い評判を得る方法は，自分自身が望む姿になるよう努めることだ。

18. 信頼するな。あなたのあらゆる言動を褒める人を。信頼するなら，わざわざ間違いを指摘してくれる人だ。

19. 生きるために食べよ。食べるために生きるな。

20. 富は善行をもたらさない。しかし善行は，もたらしてくれる。富も他の全ての恵みも，そして，個人にも国家にも。

21. 討論が終わると，悪口は負けた者の道具になる。

22. 一番の最も偉大な勝利は，自分に打ち勝つことだ。

23. 人間に関することは何でも，大して心配することではない。

24. 人に親切にせよ。あなたが出会う者はみな，より厳しい闘いをしているのだから。

25. 愛に触れると，誰もが詩人になる。

26. 目は心の窓だ。

27. 人間には，三種類いる。知を愛する者，名誉を愛する者，そして，利得を愛する者だ。

28. 賢者は話す。話すべきことがあるから。愚者は話す。話さずにはいられないから。

29. 恋という狂気は，神々から授けられる最大の恵みだ。

30. 子供を暴力と厳しさで教え込むな。その興味を用いて導け。そうすれば，分かってくる。子供の才能がどこにあるか。

31. 科学は，知覚以外の何物でもない。

32. どんな仕事も，その最初が肝心だ。

33. リズムとハーモニーは，魂の最も深いところにつながる。

34. 音楽は，世界に魂を与え，精神を自由にし，想像力をたくましくさせ，あらゆるものに命を与える。

35. 結局，死者だけが戦争の終わりを見たということになる。

36. 友をたくさん持つことは，友を一人も持たないことと同じだ。

37. 誰もが，生まれながらに知識を求める。

38. 誰でも怒ることはできる。それは簡単だ。しかし，正しい人に，正しい程度に，正しい時に，正しい目的で，そして，正しい方法で怒ることは，簡単ではない。

39. 引っ込み思案は，若者には美徳となるが，年配の者には欠点となる。

40. 勇気は人間の第一の資質だ。なぜなら，他の資質の基礎となる資質だから。

41. 威厳とは，名誉を得ているという事にではなく，名誉に値するという事にある。

42. 優秀さとは，芸術だ。訓練と習慣によって得られる。我々は，美徳と優秀さを持っているから正しく行動するのではなく，正しく行動するから美徳と優秀さを持っている。

43. ツバメが一羽来ても夏にはならないし，一日で夏になることもない。同様に，一日，あるいは，短時間で，人は恵まれたり，幸せになったりしない。

44. できるようになる前に学ばなければならいことは，実際に行なって学ぶものだ。

45. 友情とは，一つの魂だ。二つの体に宿る。

2 哲学者 (1) 解答

1. By all means marry; if you get (**a**)[1] good wife, you'll be happy. If you (**get**)[2] a bad one, you'll become a philosopher.

2. Death may be (**the**)[3] greatest of all human blessings.

3. Do not do (**to**)[4] others what angers you if done to (**you**)[5] by others.

4. Employ your time in improving yourself by other men's writings, (**so**)[6] that you shall gain easily what others have labored (**hard**)[7] for.

5. Envy is the ulcer of (**the**)[8] soul.

6. Having the fewest wants, I am nearest to (**the**)[9] gods.

7. He is richest who is content with (**the**)[10] least, for content is the wealth of nature.

8. I (**am**)[11] not an Athenian or a Greek, but (**a**)[12] citizen of the world.

9. I know nothing except the (**fact**)[13] of my ignorance.

10. If a man (**is**)[14] proud of his wealth, he should not be praised until (**it**)[15] is known how he employs it.

11. Let (**him**)[16] who would move the world, first move himself.

12. Remember that there (**is**)[17] nothing stable in human affairs; therefore avoid undue elation in prosperity, or undue depression in adversity.

13. The (**hour**)[18] of departure has arrived, and we go (**our**)[19] ways—I to die and (**you**)[20] to live. Which is the better, only God knows.

14. (**The**)[21] only good is knowledge and the (**only**)[22] evil is ignorance.

15. The only true wisdom (**is**)[23] in knowing you know nothing.

16. The unexamined life (**is**)[24] not worth living.

17. The way to gain (**a**)[25] good reputation is to endeavor to be (**what**)[26] you desire to appear.

18. Think not those faithful who praise all (**your**)[27] words and actions; but those who kindly reprove your faults.

19. You should (**eat**)[28] to live; not live to (**eat**)[29].

20. Wealth does not bring goodness, but goodness brings wealth and every other blessing, both (**to**)[30] the individual and to the state.

21. When (**the**)[31] debate is over, slander becomes the tool of (**the**)[32] loser.

22. The first and best victory is to conquer (**self**)[33].

23. Nothing in the affairs of men is worthy (**of**)[34] great anxiety.

24. Be kind, for everyone you meet (**is**)[35] fighting a harder battle.

25. At the touch of love, everyone becomes (**a**)^{36} poet.

26. The eyes are the windows (**of**)^{37} the soul.

27. There are three classes of men; lovers (**of**)^{38} wisdom, lovers of honor, and lovers of gain.

28. Wise (**men**)^{39} speak because they have something to say; Fools because they (**have**)^{40} to say something.

29. The madness of love (**is**)^{41} the greatest of heaven's blessings.

30. Do not train a child (**to**)^{42} learn by force or harshness; but direct them to (**it**)^{43} by what amuses their minds, so that you (**may**)^{44} be better able to discover with accuracy the peculiar (**bent**)^{45} of the genius of each.

31. Science is nothing (**but**)^{46} perception.

32. The beginning is the most important part (**of**)^{47} the work.

33. Rhythm and harmony find their way (**into**)^{48} the inward places of the soul.

34. Music gives a (**soul**)^{49} to the universe, wings to the mind, flight to (**the**)^{50} imagination and life to everything.

35. Only the (**dead**)^{51} have seen the end of (**war**)^{52}.

36. A friend to all is a friend (**to**)^{53} none.

37. All men by nature desire knowledge.

38. Anyone can become angry—(**that**)^{54} is easy. But to be angry (**with**)^{55} the right person, to the right degree, at the right (**time**)^{56}, for the right purpose, and in the right (**way**)^{57}—this is not easy.

39. Bashfulness is (**an**)^{58} ornament to youth, but a reproach to old (**age**)^{59}.

40. Courage is the first of human qualities because it is (**the**)^{60} quality which guarantees the others.

41. Dignity does not consist in possessing honors, but (**in**)^{61} deserving them.

42. Excellence is an art won (**by**)^{62} training and habituation. We do not act rightly because (**we**)^{63} have virtue or excellence, but we rather have those because (**we**)^{64} have acted rightly.

43. For one swallow does not make (**a**)^{65} summer, nor does one day; and so (**too**)^{66} one day, or a short time, does (**not**)^{67} make a man blessed and happy.

44. For (**the**)^{68} things we have to learn before we can (**do**)^{69} them, we learn by doing them.

45. Friendship is (**a**)^{70} single soul dwelling in two bodies.

3　作家 (1)

1-29 William Shakespeare/ウィリアム・シェイクスピア (1564 年〜1616 年)
30-45 Mark Twain/マーク・トゥエイン (1835 年〜1910 年)

CD を聞きながら，(　　　　　　　　) の中に，4 文字以下の英単語を入れて下さい。

1. A fool thinks himself to be wise, (　　　　　)[1] a wise man knows himself to be

   (　　　　　)[2] fool.

2. All the world is a stage, (　　　　　)[3] all the men and women merely players:

   They (　　　　　)[4] their exits and their entrances; And one man in his

   (　　　　　)[5] plays many parts, His acts being seven ages.

3. Brevity is (　　　　　)[6] soul of wit.

4. Cowards die many times before their deaths; (　　　　　)[7] valiant never taste of

   death but once.

5. Expectation is the (　　　　　)[8] of all heartache.

6. Give every man your (　　　　　)[9], but few your voice; Take each man's

   censure, (　　　　　)[10] reserve your judgement.

7. Glory is like a circle in (　　　　　)[11] water, Which never ceases to enlarge

   itself.　Till, by broad spreading it disperses to nought.

8. (　　　　　)[12] far that little candle throws his beams!　So shines a (　　　　　)[13]

   deed in a naughty world.

9. Life is (　　　　　)[14] tedious as a twice-told tale.

10. Life is (　　　　　)[15] a walking shadow.

11. Love is blind, and lovers cannot see (　　　　　)[16] pretty follies that themselves

    commit.

12. Love like a shadow flies when substance ( )[17] pursues; Pursuing that that flies, and flying what pursues.

13. Love sought ( )[18] good, but given unsought, is better.

14. Most subject is ( )[19] fattest soil to weeds.

15. Neither a borrower nor a lender ( )[20]; For loan oft loses both itself and friend, ( )[21] borrowing dulls the edge of husbandry.

16. One sorrow never comes but brings an ( )[22]. That may succeed as his inheritor.

17. Poor ( )[23] content is rich and rich enough; but riches endless ( )[24] as poor and winter to him ( )[25] ever fears he shall be poor.

18. Present fears are ( )[26] than horrible imaginings.

19. So may the outward shows be least themselves: The world is still deceived with ornament.

20. Sweet ( )[27] the uses of adversity, Which, like the ( )[28], ugly and venomous, Wears yet a precious jewel in ( )[29] head.

21. The better for my foes ( )[30] the worse for my friends.

22. The labor we delight ( )[31] cures pain.

23. The miserable have no other medicine but ( )[32] hope.

24. The worst is not, so ( )[33] as we can say, 'This ( )[34] the worst.'

3 作家（1）

25. There is a tide in (   )^{35} affairs of men. Which, taken at the flood,

    leads on (   )^{36} fortune; Omitted, all the voyage of their life is bound

    (   )^{37} shallows and in miseries.

26. There is nothing either good or (   )^{38}, but thinking makes it so.

27. To be, (   )^{39} not to be: that is (   )^{40} question.

28. Women are as roses, whose fairflower being once displayed, does fall

    (   )^{41} very hour.

29. You gods, will give (   )^{42} some faults to make us men.

30. (   )^{43} lie can travel half way around the world while (   )^{44}

    truth is putting on its shoes.

31. A person with (   )^{45} new idea is a crank until the (   )^{46} suc-

    ceeds.

32. All you need in this (   )^{47} is ignorance and confidence, and then suc-

    cess is (   )^{48}.

33. Courage is resistance to fear, mastery of fear—(   )^{49} absence of fear.

34. Education: the path from cocky ignorance (   )^{50} miserable uncertainty.

35. Everyone is a moon, and has (   )^{51} dark side which he never shows to

    anybody.

36. Foreigners always spell better than (   )^{52} pronounce.

37. Forgiveness is the fragrance that the violet sheds on (   )^{53} heel that has

    crushed it.

38. Good friends, (　　　　　　)^{54} books and a sleepy conscience: this is the ideal

(　　　　　)^{55}.

39. He liked to like people, therefore people liked him.

40. I (　　　　　)^{56} live for two months on a good compliment.

41. (　　　　　)^{57} don't mind what the opposition say of (　　　　　)^{58} so long as

they don't tell (　　　　　)^{59} truth about me.

42. I was gratified to be (　　　　　)^{60} to answer promptly.　I said I don't know.

43. (　　　　　)^{61} you tell the truth, you don't have (　　　　　)^{62} remember any-

thing.

44. It is a good idea (　　　　　)^{63} obey all the rules when you're young just

(　　　　　)^{64} you'll have the strength to break them when you're

(　　　　　)^{65}.

45. It usually takes me more than three weeks to prepare (　　　　　)^{66} good

impromptu speech.

3 作家（1）日本語訳

問題英文の日本語訳を確認しよう。

1. 愚者は自分が賢いと思っているが，賢者は自分が愚かであることを知っている。

2. 全世界は一つの舞台で，すべての男女は，その役者にすぎない。それぞれ舞台に登場しては，退場していく。人はその時々にさまざまな役を演じる。舞台は年齢によって七幕に分かれている。

3. 簡潔さ。それが，知恵の真髄だ。

4. 臆病者は，実際に死ぬまでに何度も死ぬが，勇者は，一度しか死を経験しない。

5. 期待はあらゆる苦悩のもとだ。

6. 誰の話も聞いてやれ，しかし自分のことはあまり話すな。他人の非難をよく聞け，しかし自分の判断は控えよ。

7. 栄光は水面の輪のようなものだ。輪が広がりすぎて消えてしまうまで，大きくなり続けるのを止めないからだ。

8. あの小さなろうそくが，なんと遠くまで照らすことか！同様に，善行も，愚かな世界で光る。

9. 人生は，退屈だ。二度繰り返される物語と同じほど。

10. 人生は，運命に従って行動するだけの，ついてまわる影法師にすぎない。

11. 恋は盲目だ。恋人たちは，自分たちが犯す小さな愚行が見えなくなる。

12. 恋は，影法師のように，追いかけても逃げて行く。追いかければ逃げ，逃げれば追いかけてくるものだ。

13. 求めて得られた恋も良いが，求めずに得られた恋は，なお良い。

14. 肥えた土ほど，雑草は育つ。

15. 金の貸し借りをするな。金を貸せば金も友も失う。金を借りれば節約する気がなくなる。

16. 悲しみは独りではやって来ない。必ず後継ぎと一緒にやって来る。その悲しみを引き継いでくれる者と共に。

17. 貧しくても満足している人間は豊かだ。しかも，相当豊かだ。しかし，大金を持っていても，貧しく，冬枯れのようなものだ。いつ貧しくなるかと恐れている人間は。

18. 眼前の恐怖は，想像力による恐怖ほどではない。

19. 外観は，まったく何も知らせてくれないかもしれない。この世界は，依然，飾り付けにだまされている。

20. 逆境は，うまく使う価値がある。逆境は，ヒキガエルに似て，醜く，毒を含んでいるが，頭の中には宝石を持っている。

21. 敵のおかげでいい目に遭い，友のおかげで悪い目に遭う。

22. 苦労を楽しんでやれば，苦痛も癒える。

23. みじめな気持ちを治す薬は，希望しかない。

24. まだそれは最悪ではない。「これが最悪だ」と言えるうちは。

25. 人が成すことには潮時がある。うまく満ち潮に乗れば成功するが，その期を逃すと，一生の航海が，浅瀬につかまり，ひどい目に遭う。

26. 物事に良いも悪いもない。考え方次第で，良くも悪くもなる。

27. 生きるべきか，死ぬべきか。それが問うべき問いだ。

28. 女はバラに似ている。ひとたび咲いたら，それは散る時だ。

29. 神々は，我々を人間にするために，何らかの欠点を与える。

30. 嘘は世界を半周する。真実が靴を履こうとしている間に。

31. 新しい考えを思いついた人も，ただの変わり者だ。それが成功するまでは。

32. 人生で必要なものは無知と自信だけだ。これだけあれば，成功がついてくる。

33. 勇気とは，恐怖に抵抗し，恐怖を克服することで，恐怖を抱かないことではない。

34. 教育とは，こんな道だ。うぬぼれた無知からみじめな不確実さへの。

35. 人間は誰もが月だ。誰にも見せない闇を持っているから。

36. 外国人は，決まって，発音は下手だが，綴りは正確だ。

37. 許しとは，香りだ。スミレの花が，自分を踏みつけたかかとに放つ。

38. 親友，良書，眠りかけの良心，これは，理想の人生だ。

39. 彼は，人のことが好きになることが好きだった。だから，人は彼のことが好きだった。

40. 2ヶ月はそれで生きられる。いいお世辞を言ってもらえれば。

41. 私に批判的な人が私のことを何と言おうとかまわない。彼らが私について真実を語らない限りは。

42. 私は即座に答えることができて嬉しかった。「私は知らない」と言ってやった。

43. 真実を話すなら，何も覚えておく必要がない。

44. 若いうちは，どんな規則にも従っておくのが良い。歳をとれば，規則を破る力を手に入れるのだから。

45. 大抵3週間以上かかる。使える即席のスピーチを準備するには。

3 作家（1）解答

1. A fool thinks himself to be wise, (**but**)[1] a wise man knows himself to be (**a**)[2] fool.

2. All the world is a stage, (**And**)[3] all the men and women merely players: They (**have**)[4] their exits and their entrances; And one man in his (**time**)[5] plays many parts, His acts being seven ages.

3. Brevity is (**the**)[6] soul of wit.

4. Cowards die many times before their deaths; (**The**)[7] valiant never taste of death but once.

5. Expectation is the (**root**)[8] of all heartache.

6. Give every man your (**ear**)[9], but few your voice; Take each man's censure, (**but**)[10] reserve your judgement.

7. Glory is like a circle in (**the**)[11] water, Which never ceases to enlarge itself. Till, by broad spreading it disperses to nought.

8. (**How**)[12] far that little candle throws his beams! So shines a (**good**)[13] deed in a naughty world.

9. Life is (**as**)[14] tedious as a twice-told tale.

10. Life is (**but**)[15] a walking shadow.

11. Love is blind, and lovers cannot see (**the**)[16] pretty follies that themselves commit.

12. Love like a shadow flies when substance (**love**)[17] pursues; Pursuing that that flies, and flying what pursues.

13. Love sought (**is**)[18] good, but given unsought, is better.

14. Most subject is (**the**)[19] fattest soil to weeds.

15. Neither a borrower nor a lender (**be**)[20]; For loan oft loses both itself and friend, (**And**)[21] borrowing dulls the edge of husbandry.

16. One sorrow never comes but brings an (**heir**)[22]. That may succeed as his inheritor.

17. Poor (**and**)[23] content is rich and rich enough; but riches endless (**is**)[24] as poor and winter to him (**that**)[25] ever fears he shall be poor.

18. Present fears are (**less**)[26] than horrible imaginings.

19. So may the outward shows be least themselves: The world is still deceived with ornament.

20. Sweet (**are**)[27] the uses of adversity, Which, like the (**toad**)[28], ugly and venomous, Wears yet a precious jewel in (**his**)[29] head.

21. The better for my foes (**and**)[30] the worse for my friends.

22. The labor we delight (**in**)[31] cures pain.

23. The miserable have no other medicine but (**only**)^{32} hope.

24. The worst is not, so (**long**)^{33} as we can say, 'This (**is**)^{34} the worst.'

25. There is a tide in (**the**)^{35} affairs of men. Which, taken at the flood, leads on (**to**)^{36} fortune; Omitted, all the voyage of their life is bound (**in**)^{37} shallows and in miseries.

26. There is nothing either good or (**bad**)^{38}, but thinking makes it so.

27. To be, (**or**)^{39} not to be: that is (**the**)^{40} question.

28. Women are as roses, whose fairflower being once displayed, does fall (**that**)^{41} very hour.

29. You gods, will give (**us**)^{42} some faults to make us men.

30. (**A**)^{43} lie can travel half way around the world while (**the**)^{44} truth is putting on its shoes.

31. A person with (**a**)^{45} new idea is a crank until the (**idea**)^{46} succeeds.

32. All you need in this (**life**)^{47} is ignorance and confidence, and then success is (**sure**)^{48}.

33. Courage is resistance to fear, mastery of fear— (**not**)^{49} absence of fear.

34. Education: the path from cocky ignorance (**to**)^{50} miserable uncertainty.

35. Everyone is a moon, and has (**a**)^{51} dark side which he never shows to anybody.

36. Foreigners always spell better than (**they**)^{52} pronounce.

37. Forgiveness is the fragrance that the violet sheds on (**the**)^{53} heel that has crushed it.

38. Good friends, (**good**)^{54} books and a sleepy conscience: this is the ideal (**life**)^{55}.

39. He liked to like people, therefore people liked him.

40. I (**can**)^{56} live for two months on a good compliment.

41. (**I**)^{57} don't mind what the opposition say of (**me**)^{58} so long as they don't tell (**the**)^{59} truth about me.

42. I was gratified to be (**able**)^{60} to answer promptly. I said I don't know.

43. (**If**)^{61} you tell the truth, you don't have (**to**)^{62} remember anything.

44. It is a good idea (**to**)^{63} obey all the rules when you're young just (**so**)^{64} you'll have the strength to break them when you're (**old**)^{65}.

45. It usually takes me more than three weeks to prepare (**a**)^{66} good impromptu speech.

4 芸術家 (1)

1-14 Leonardo da Vinci/レオナルド・ダ・ヴィンチ (1452 年〜1519 年)
15-34 Michelangelo Buonarroti/ミケランジェロ・ブオナローティ (1475 年〜1564 年)
35-44 Vincent van Gogh/フィンセント・ファン・ゴッホ (1853 年〜1890 年)
45 Wolfgang Amadeus Mozart/ヴォルフガング・アマデウス・モーツァルト (1756 年〜1791 年)

CD を聞きながら，（　　　　　　　　　）の中に，4 文字以下の英単語を入れて下さい。

1. A good painter is to paint two main things, namely, (　　　　　　)^1 and the workings of man's mind.

2. Anyone who conducts (　　　　　)^2 argument by appealing to authority is not
   using his intelligence; (　　　　　)^3 is just using his memory.

3. Art is never finished, (　　　　)^4 abandoned.

4. As a well-spent day brings happy sleep, so life (　　　　)^5 used brings happy
   death.

5. He who does not punish (　　　　)^6 commands that it be done.

6. In rivers, (　　　　)^7 water that you touch is the last (　　　　)^8 what has
   passed and the first of (　　　　)^9 which comes; so with present time.

7. Iron rusts from disuse; stagnant water loses (　　　　)^{10} purity and in cold
   weather becomes frozen; even so (　　　　)^{11} inaction sap the vigor of the
   mind.

8. (　　　　)^{12} as eating against one's will is injurious to health, so studying
   without (　　　　)^{13} liking for it spoils the memory, and it retains nothing
   (　　　　)^{14} takes in.

9. Simplicity is the ultimate sophistication.

10. The noblest pleasure is (　　　　)^{15} joy of understanding.

11. The poet ranks far below (   )¹⁶ painter in the representation of visible things, and far below (   )¹⁷ musician in that of invisible things.

12. The smallest feline is (   )¹⁸ masterpiece.

13. Where the spirit does not work with (   )¹⁹ hand, there is no art.

14. Wisdom is (   )²⁰ daughter of experience.

15. A man paints with his brains (   )²¹ not with his hands.

16. Beauty is the purgation (   )²² superfluities.

17. Death and love are the two wings that (   )²³ the good man to heaven.

18. Every block of stone (   )²⁴ a statue inside it and it is (   )²⁵ task of the sculptor to discover it.

19. Genius (   )²⁶ eternal patience.

20. Good painting is the kind that looks (   )²⁷ sculpture.

21. I am a poor man (   )²⁸ of little worth, who is laboring in that (   )²⁹ that God has given me in order to extend (   )³⁰ life as long as possible.

22. I (   )³¹ and love in God's peculiar light.

23. I saw (   )³² angel in the marble and carved until I set (   )³³ free.

24. If people knew how hard (   )³⁴ had to work to gain (   )³⁵ mastery, it would not seem so wonderful at (   )³⁶.

4 芸術家 (1)

25. If you knew how much (　　　　)[37] went into it, you would not

(　　　　)[38] it genius.

26. It is necessary to keep one's compass (　　　　)[39] one's eyes and not in the

(　　　　)[40], for the hands execute, but the eye judges.

27. Lord, grant (　　　　)[41] I may always desire more than I (　　　　)[42]

accomplish.

28. My soul can find no staircase (　　　　)[43] Heaven unless it be through Earth's

loveliness.

29. The greatest danger for most (　　　　)[44] us is not that our (　　　　)[45] is

too high and we (　　　　)[46] it, but that it is (　　　　)[47] low and we reach

it.

30. The marble (　　　　)[48] yet carved can hold the form (　　　　)[49] every

thought the greatest artist has.

31. The more the marbles wastes, (　　　　)[50] more the statue grows.

32. The true work (　　　　)[51] art is but a shadow of (　　　　)[52] divine per-

fection.

33. There is no greater harm than that (　　　　)[53] time wasted.

34. Trifles make perfection, but perfection is no trifle.

35. (　　　　)[54] not quench your inspiration and your imagination; do

(　　　　)[55] become the slave of your model.

36. Great things are not (   )^{56} by impulse, but by a series of small things

brought together.

37. (   )^{57} am always doing what I can't do yet, (   )^{58} order to

learn how to do it.

38. (   )^{59} envy the Japanese the extreme clarity in whatever they

(   )^{60}.

39. I put my heart and my (   )^{61} into my work, and have (   )^{62}

my mind in the process.

40. Love (   )^{63} something eternal; the aspect may change, but not the

essence.

41. (   )^{64} best way to know God is (   )^{65} love many things.

42. The more I think about (   )^{66}, the more I realize there is nothing more

artistic (   )^{67} to love others.

43. There is no blue without yellow (   )^{68} without orange.

44. Your life would be very empty if (   )^{69} had nothing to regret.

45. Believe me, I do (   )^{70} like idleness but work.

4 芸術家 (1) 日本語訳

問題英文の日本語訳を確認しよう。

1. 優れた画家は二つのものを描く。人と人の心の動きだ。

2. 議論をするのに権威を持ち出す人は，知性を使っているのではない。記憶力を使っているだけだ。

3. 芸術は，決して完成しない。途中で放り出されただけだ。

4. 一日が充実していれば，幸せな眠りが得られるように，一生が充実していれば，幸せな死が得られる。

5. 悪を罰しない者は，悪をなせと命じているようなものだ。

6. 川に行って，あなたが触る水は，一番最後に過ぎ去ったもので，かつ，一番最初にやって来るものだ。「今」という時も同じだ。

7. 鉄は使わなければ錆びる。水は澱んでいれば濁り，冷えてくれば凍る。同様に，怠惰でいれば気力も失われる。

8. 食欲がないのに食べても健康に悪いように，やる気がないのに勉強しても記憶力がだいなしになり，何も記憶できない。

9. シンプルさは究極の洗練だ。

10. 最も高貴な楽しみは，理解する喜びだ。

11. 詩人は，目に見える表現の中では画家よりもはるか下に見られ，目に見えぬ表現の中では音楽家よりもはるか下に見られる。

12. 一番小さな猫科の動物，つまり猫は，最高傑作だ。

13. 魂が手とともに働かなければ，芸術など存在しない。

14. 知恵は経験の娘である。

15. 絵は頭で描くもので，手で描くものではない。

16. 美は，余計なものを浄化したものだ。

17. 死と愛は，善人を天国に運ぶ両翼だ。

18. どんな石の塊も内部に彫像を秘め，それを発見するのが彫刻家の仕事だ。

19. 天才は，永遠に忍耐ができる才能だ。

20. 優れた絵画は，彫刻のように見えるものだ。

21. 私は，貧しく価値のない人間だ。ただ，神が私に与えてくれた芸術分野で働き，できる限り自分の命を永らえようとしている。

22. 私は，神の特別な光の中で生き，そして愛する。

23. 私は大理石の中に天使を見，その天使が自由になるまで彫った。

24. 私がこの芸術の域に達するまでに，どれほど頑張ったかを知ったら，素晴らしいことのようにはとても見えないだろう。

25. どれだけの労力を注ぎ込んだかを知れば，天才なんて呼べないはずだ。

26. 羅針盤は，目の中に持つことが必要だ。手の中にではなく。手が実行し，目が判断するのだから。

27. 神よ，私がいつも，成し得る以上のことを望むことをお許しください。

28. 私の魂は，天国への階段を見つけることができない。地球のいとおしさを通るまでは。

29. ほとんどの人間にとって，最大の危機は，目標が高すぎて達成しないことではなく，目標が低すぎて達成してしまうことだ。

30. まだ彫られていない大理石は，最も偉大な芸術家が考えつくすべての形状を持ちうる。

31. 大理石の余分な部分がそぎ落とされればそぎ落されるほど，彫像は成長する。

32. 真の芸術作品は，神がもたらす完成の影そのものだ。

33. 時間を浪費するほど大きな害はない。

34. 些細なことが完璧を生むが，完璧は決して些細なことではない。

35. あなたが持つインスピレーションやイマジネーションを抑えてはならない。自分が勝手に決めた模範の奴隷になるな。

36. 偉業は，一時の衝動でなされず，些細なことの積み重ねによってなされる。

37. 私はいつも，まだ自分ができないことをしている。そのし方を学ぶために。

38. 日本人が何をするにも明確であることが，羨ましい。

39. 私は，自分の作品に心と魂を込め，制作過程で我を失う。

40. 愛は永遠なものだ。形が変わることはあるが，本質は変わらない。

41. 神を知る最善の方法は，多くの物を愛することだ。

42. 考えれば考えるほど，人を愛すること以上に芸術的なものは何もないということに気づく。

43. 黄色とオレンジ色がなければ，青色もない。

44. あなたの人生はとても空虚なものになるだろう。後悔することがなければ。

45. これは本当だ。私は怠けることが嫌いで，働くことが好きだ。

4 芸術家（1）解答

1. A good painter is to paint two main things, namely, (**man**)[1] and the workings of man's mind.

2. Anyone who conducts (**an**)[2] argument by appealing to authority is not using his intelligence; (**he**)[3] is just using his memory.

3. Art is never finished, (**only**)[4] abandoned.

4. As a well-spent day brings happy sleep, so life (**well**)[5] used brings happy death.

5. He who does not punish (**evil**)[6] commands that it be done.

6. In rivers, (**the**)[7] water that you touch is the last (**of**)[8] what has passed and the first of (**that**)[9] which comes; so with present time.

7. Iron rusts from disuse; stagnant water loses (**its**)[10] purity and in cold weather becomes frozen; even so (**does**)[11] inaction sap the vigor of the mind.

8. (**Just**)[12] as eating against one's will is injurious to health, so studying without (**a**)[13] liking for it spoils the memory, and it retains nothing (**it**)[14] takes in.

9. Simplicity is the ultimate sophistication.

10. The noblest pleasure is (**the**)[15] joy of understanding.

11. The poet ranks far below (**the**)[16] painter in the representation of visible things, and far below (**the**)[17] musician in that of invisible things.

12. The smallest feline is (**a**)[18] masterpiece.

13. Where the spirit does not work with (**the**)[19] hand, there is no art.

14. Wisdom is (**the**)[20] daughter of experience.

15. A man paints with his brains (**and**)[21] not with his hands.

16. Beauty is the purgation (**of**)[22] superfluities.

17. Death and love are the two wings that (**bear**)[23] the good man to heaven.

18. Every block of stone (**has**)[24] a statue inside it and it is (**the**)[25] task of the sculptor to discover it.

19. Genius (**is**)[26] eternal patience.

20. Good painting is the kind that looks (**like**)[27] sculpture.

21. I am a poor man (**and**)[28] of little worth, who is laboring in that (**art**)[29] that God has given me in order to extend (**my**)[30] life as long as possible.

22. I (**live**)[31] and love in God's peculiar light.

23. I saw (**the**)[32] angel in the marble and carved until I set (**him**)[33] free.

24. If people knew how hard (**I**)[34] had to work to gain (**my**)[35] mastery, it would not seem so

wonderful at (**all**)[36].

25. If you knew how much (**work**)[37] went into it, you would not (**call**)[38] it genius.

26. It is necessary to keep one's compass (**in**)[39] one's eyes and not in the (**hand**)[40], for the hands execute, but the eye judges.

27. Lord, grant (**that**)[41] I may always desire more than I (**can**)[42] accomplish.

28. My soul can find no staircase (**to**)[43] Heaven unless it be through Earth's loveliness.

29. The greatest danger for most (**of**)[44] us is not that our (**aim**)[45] is too high and we (**miss**)[46] it, but that it is (**too**)[47] low and we reach it.

30. The marble (**not**)[48] yet carved can hold the form (**of**)[49] every thought the greatest artist has.

31. The more the marbles wastes, (**the**)[50] more the statue grows.

32. The true work (**of**)[51] art is but a shadow of (**the**)[52] divine perfection.

33. There is no greater harm than that (**of**)[53] time wasted.

34. Trifles make perfection, but perfection is no trifle.

35. (**Do**)[54] not quench your inspiration and your imagination; do (**not**)[55] become the slave of your model.

36. Great things are not (**done**)[56] by impulse, but by a series of small things brought together.

37. (**I**)[57] am always doing what I can't do yet, (**in**)[58] order to learn how to do it.

38. (**I**)[59] envy the Japanese the extreme clarity in whatever they (**do**)[60].

39. I put my heart and my (**soul**)[61] into my work, and have (**lost**)[62] my mind in the process.

40. Love (**is**)[63] something eternal; the aspect may change, but not the essence.

41. (**The**)[64] best way to know God is (**to**)[65] love many things.

42. The more I think about (**it**)[66], the more I realize there is nothing more artistic (**than**)[67] to love others.

43. There is no blue without yellow (**and**)[68] without orange.

44. Your life would be very empty if (**you**)[69] had nothing to regret.

45. Believe me, I do (**not**)[70] like idleness but work.

5　実業家（1）

1–27 Henry Ford/ヘンリー・フォード（1863 年～1947 年）
28–45 Thomas Edison/トーマス・エジソン（1847 年～1931 年）

CD を聞きながら，（　　　　　　　　）の中に，4 文字以下の英単語を入れて下さい。

1. A business that makes nothing but money is a (　　　　　　)^1 business.

2. An idealist is a person who helps other people to (　　　　　　)^2 prosperous.

3. Anyone who stops learning is old, whether at 20 or 80.　Anyone (　　　　　　)^3 keeps learning stays young.　The greatest thing in life is to (　　　　　　)^4 your mind young.

4. Before everything else, getting ready is the secret (　　　　　　)^5 success.

5. Business is never so healthy as when, like (　　　　　　)^6 chicken, it must do a certain amount of scratching (　　　　　　)^7 what it gets.

6. Chop your (　　　　　　)^8 wood, and it will warm (　　　　　　)^9 twice.

7. Don't find fault, find a remedy; anybody can complain.

8. Failure is simply (　　　　　　)^{10} opportunity to begin again, this time more intelligently.　There is (　　　　　　)^{11} disgrace in honest failure; there is disgrace in fearing to fail.

9. (　　　　　　)^{12} there is any one secret of success, it lies (　　　　　　)^{13} the ability to get the other person's point of (　　　　　　)^{14} and see things from that person's angle as (　　　　　　)^{15} as from your own.

10. Indecision is often worse (　　　　　　)^{16} wrong action.

11. It has been my observation that (　　　　　　)^{17} people get ahead during the time that others waste.

12. It (　　　　　)^{18} not the employer who pays the wages. Employers (　　　　　)^{19} handle the money. It is the customer who (　　　　　)^{20} the wages.

13. Money is like an arm (　　　　　)^{21} a leg—use it or (　　　　　)^{22} it.

14. Most people spend more time and energy going around problems (　　　　　)^{23} in trying to solve them.

15. My best friend (　　　　　)^{24} the one who brings out the best (　　　　　)^{25} me.

16. Nothing is particularly hard if you divide (　　　　　)^{26} into small jobs.

17. Obstacles are those frightful things you see (　　　　　)^{27} you take your eyes off (　　　　　)^{28} goals.

18. Old men are always advising young men to (　　　　　)^{29} money. That is bad advice. Don't save every nickel. Invest in yourself. (　　　　　)^{30} never saved a dollar until I was 40 years old.

19. One of (　　　　　)^{31} greatest discoveries a man makes, one of his great surprises, is (　　　　　)^{32} find he can do what (　　　　　)^{33} was afraid he couldn't do.

20. Quality means doing it right when (　　　　　)^{34} one is looking.

21. The competitor to be feared is one (　　　　　)^{35} never bothers about you at all, but goes (　　　　　)^{36} making his own business better all the time.

22. (　　　　　)^{37} highest use of capital is not to (　　　　　)^{38} more money, but to make money do (　　　　　)^{39} for the betterment of life.

23. There is (   )[40] in work. There is no happiness except in
    (   )[41] realization that we have accomplished something.

24. There is no (   )[42] living who isn't capable of doing more than he thinks
    (   )[43] can do.

25. Thinking is the hardest work there (   )[44], which is probably the reason
    why so few engage (   )[45] it.

26. Whether you believe you can do (   )[46] thing or not, you are right.

27. You can't build (   )[47] reputation on what you are going to
    (   )[48].

28. All Bibles are man-made.

29. Everything comes to him who hustles while (   )[49] waits.

30. From his neck down a (   )[50] is worth a couple of dollars a day,
    (   )[51] his neck up he is worth anything (   )[52] his brain can
    produce.

31. Genius is 1 percent inspiration and 99 percent perspiration.

32. I (   )[53] not discouraged, because every wrong attempt discarded is
    another step forward.

33. I find (   )[54] what the world needs. Then, I go ahead (   )[55]
    invent it.

34. I have not failed. I've just found 10,000 (   )[56] that won't work.

35. I never did a day's (   )[57] in my life. It was (   )[58] fun.

36. I owe my success to (   )[59] fact that I never had a clock (   )[60]
    my workroom.

37. If we did all (   )^{61} things we are capable of doing, we would literally astound ourselves.

38. Just because something doesn't (   )^{62} what you planned it to do doesn't (   )^{63} it's useless.

39. Many of life's failures are people who did (   )^{64} realize how close they were to success when (   )^{65} gave up.

40. Nearly every person who develops an idea works (   )^{66} it up to the point where it looks impossible, (   )^{67} then gets discouraged. That's not the place to become discouraged.

41. (   )^{68} greatest weakness lies in giving up. The most certain (   )^{69} to succeed is always to try just one (   )^{70} time.

42. Show me a thoroughly satisfied man (   )^{71} I will show you a failure.

43. (   )^{72} best thinking has been done in solitude. (   )^{73} worst has been done in turmoil.

44. The first requisite (   )^{74} success is to develop the ability to focus and apply (   )^{75} mental and physical energies to the problem at hand—without growing weary.

45. There (   )^{76} no rules here—we're trying to accomplish something.

5 実業家（1）日本語訳

問題英文の日本語訳を確認しよう。

1. 金以外に何も生み出さないビジネスは，貧しいビジネスだ。

2. 理想主義者とは，他人が成功するのを助ける者だ。

3. 学ぶことをやめた者は，二十歳であろうが八十歳であろうが，老人だ。学び続ける者はいつまでも若い。人生で最も大切なことは，心を若く保つことだ。

4. 何にもまして，準備することが，成功の秘訣だ。

5. ビジネスは，次の時ほど，健全な時はない。それは，ちょうどニワトリのように，得るもののために一定の努力をしなければならない時だ。

6. 自分で薪を割れ。そうすれば，二回温まる。

7. 誤りを探さず，改善策を見つけよ。不平など誰でも言える。

8. 失敗とは，再挑戦するためのよい機会だ。今度は，より賢く。まじめな失敗は，恥ではない。失敗を恐れる心の中に，恥がある。

9. 成功の秘訣というものがあれば，それは，次の能力の内にある。つまり，他人の視点を理解し，自分の立場と同時に他人の立場からも物事を見ることができる能力だ。

10. 決断しないことは，時として，誤った行動より悪い。

11. 私が見る限り，ほとんどの成功者は他人が時間を浪費している間に先へ進む。

12. 賃金を払うのは雇い主ではない。雇い主は，ただ金を扱っているだけだ。賃金を払うのは顧客だ。

13. 金は手や足に似ている。使わなければ，失う。

14. 大抵の人は，問題を回避するためにより多くの時間とエネルギーを費やしている。問題を解決しようとするよりも。

15. 私の最高の友は，私の中から最高の私を引き出してくれる友だ。

16. どんな事も特に難しいことはない。それを小さな仕事に分けてしまえば。

17. 目の前に立ちはだかる障害物は，恐ろしいものに見えてくる。自分の目標から目を離すと。

18. 年寄りはいつも若い者に貯金をしろと言う。それはよくない助言だ。財布の中の小銭を貯めようとするな。自分に投資せよ。私は，1ドルも貯金したことなどなかった。40歳になるまで。

19. 一人の人間にとっての最大の発見，かつ，最大の驚きは，自分にはできないと思っていたことが，実はできると知ることだ。

20. ものごとの質とは，きちっとやることだ。誰も見ていない時に。

21. 恐るべき競争相手とは，あなたのことをまったく気にかけず，自分の仕事を常に向上させ続け

る人間だ。

22. 資本の真の使い方は，金を増やすことではく，金を増やして，生活を向上させることだ。

23. 仕事の中に喜びがある。幸せなどない。何かを達成したという実感なしには。

24. こんな人間は，一人もいない。自分が思っている以上のことができない人間は。

25. 考えることは最も大変な仕事だ。それだからおそらく，それをやろうとする人がほとんどいない。

26. あなたができると思えばでき，できないと思えばできない。どちらにしても，あなたは正しい。

27. これからやろうとしていることでは，名声は得られない。

28. 権威がある本と言っても，所詮，人が書いたものだ。

29. すべてのものが得られるのは，待っている間も頑張る人だ。

30. 首から下で稼げるのは 1 日数ドルだが，首から上を働かせればいくらでも富を生み出せる。

31. 天才という才能は，1%のひらめきと 99%の努力だ。

32. 私は，失望などしない。どんな失敗も，新たな一歩となるからだ。

33. 世界が必要としているものを見つけ出す。そして，先へ進み，それを発明する。

34. 私は失敗したことがない。1 万通りの，うまく行かない方法を見つけてきただけだ。

35. 私は一日も，労働などしたことがない。何をやっても楽しかったからだ。

36. 私が成功したのは，仕事場に時計がなかったからだ。

37. 我々が自分にできることを全て行えば，文字通り，自分自身に驚いてしまうだろう。

38. 作ったものが計画通りに動かないからといって，それが無駄だとは限らない。

39. 人生に失敗した人の多くは，こんな人たちだ。それは，諦めた時に，どれほど成功に近づいていたか気づかなかった人たちだ。

40. ほとんどすべての人間は，もうこれ以上アイデアを出すのは不可能だというところまで行き，そこで諦めてしまう。そこは，諦めどころではないのに。

41. 私たちの最大の弱点は諦めることにある。成功するのに最も確かな方法は，常にもう一回だけ試してみることだ。

42. 完全に満足しきった人がいたら，逢わせてくれ。そうでないことをお見せしよう。

43. 最高の思考は孤独のうちになされる。最低の思考は混乱のうちになされる。

44. 成功に不可欠なのは，集中し，手元の問題に，肉体的かつ精神的エネルギーを注ぎ込む能力だ。疲れを溜めずに。

45. ここに，規則などない。我々が何かを成し遂げようとしているところに。

5 実業家（1）解答

1. A business that makes nothing but money is a (**poor**)[1] business.

2. An idealist is a person who helps other people to (**be**)[2] prosperous.

3. Anyone who stops learning is old, whether at 20 or 80. Anyone (**who**)[3] keeps learning stays young. The greatest thing in life is to (**keep**)[4] your mind young.

4. Before everything else, getting ready is the secret (**of**)[5] success.

5. Business is never so healthy as when, like (**a**)[6] chicken, it must do a certain amount of scratching (**for**)[7] what it gets.

6. Chop your (**own**)[8] wood, and it will warm (**you**)[9] twice.

7. Don't find fault, find a remedy; anybody can complain.

8. Failure is simply (**the**)[10] opportunity to begin again, this time more intelligently. There is (**no**)[11] disgrace in honest failure; there is disgrace in fearing to fail.

9. (**If**)[12] there is any one secret of success, it lies (**in**)[13] the ability to get the other person's point of (**view**)[14] and see things from that person's angle as (**well**)[15] as from your own.

10. Indecision is often worse (**than**)[16] wrong action.

11. It has been my observation that (**most**)[17] people get ahead during the time that others waste.

12. It (**is**)[18] not the employer who pays the wages. Employers (**only**)[19] handle the money. It is the customer who (**pays**)[20] the wages.

13. Money is like an arm (**or**)[21] a leg—use it or (**lose**)[22] it.

14. Most people spend more time and energy going around problems (**than**)[23] in trying to solve them.

15. My best friend (**is**)[24] the one who brings out the best (**in**)[25] me.

16. Nothing is particularly hard if you divide (**it**)[26] into small jobs.

17. Obstacles are those frightful things you see (**when**)[27] you take your eyes off (**your**)[28] goals.

18. Old men are always advising young men to (**save**)[29] money. That is bad advice. Don't save every nickel. Invest in yourself. (**I**)[30] never saved a dollar until I was 40 years old.

19. One of (**the**)[31] greatest discoveries a man makes, one of his great surprises, is (**to**)[32] find he can do what (**he**)[33] was afraid he couldn't do.

20. Quality means doing it right when (**no**)[34] one is looking.

21. The competitor to be feared is one (**who**)[35] never bothers about you at all, but goes (**on**)[36] making his own business better all the time.

22. (**The**)[37] highest use of capital is not to (**make**)[38] more money, but to make money do (**more**)[39] for the betterment of life.

23. There is (**joy**)[40] in work.　There is no happiness except in (**the**)[41] realization that we have accomplished something.

24. There is no (**man**)[42] living who isn't capable of doing more than he thinks (**he**)[43] can do.

25. Thinking is the hardest work there (**is**)[44], which is probably the reason why so few engage (**in**)[45] it.

26. Whether you believe you can do (**a**)[46] thing or not, you are right.

27. You can't build (**a**)[47] reputation on what you are going to (**do**)[48].

28. All Bibles are man-made.

29. Everything comes to him who hustles while (**he**)[49] waits.

30. From his neck down a (**man**)[50] is worth a couple of dollars a day, (**from**)[51] his neck up he is worth anything (**that**)[52] his brain can produce.

31. Genius is 1 percent inspiration and 99 percent perspiration.

32. I (**am**)[53] not discouraged, because every wrong attempt discarded is another step forward.

33. I find (**out**)[54] what the world needs.　Then, I go ahead (**and**)[55] invent it.

34. I have not failed.　I've just found 10,000 (**ways**)[56] that won't work.

35. I never did a day's (**work**)[57] in my life.　It was (**all**)[58] fun.

36. I owe my success to (**the**)[59] fact that I never had a clock (**in**)[60] my workroom.

37. If we did all (**the**)[61] things we are capable of doing, we would literally astound ourselves.

38. Just because something doesn't (**do**)[62] what you planned it to do doesn't (**mean**)[63] it's useless.

39. Many of life's failures are people who did (**not**)[64] realize how close they were to success when (**they**)[65] gave up.

40. Nearly every person who develops an idea works (**at**)[66] it up to the point where it looks impossible, (**and**)[67] then gets discouraged.　That's not the place to become discouraged.

41. (**Our**)[68] greatest weakness lies in giving up.　The most certain (**way**)[69] to succeed is always to try just one (**more**)[70] time.

42. Show me a thoroughly satisfied man (**and**)[71] I will show you a failure.

43. (**The**)[72] best thinking has been done in solitude.　(**The**)[73] worst has been done in turmoil.

44. The first requisite (**for**)[74] success is to develop the ability to focus and apply (**your**)[75] mental and physical energies to the problem at hand—without growing weary.

45. There (**are**)[76] no rules here—we're trying to accomplish something.

6 政治家 (1)

1–23 Mahatma Gandhi/マハトマ・ガンジー（1869 年〜1948 年）
24–45 Benjamin Franklin/ベンジャミン・フランクリン（1706 年〜1790 年）

CD を聞きながら，（ 　　　　　 ）の中に，4 文字以下の英単語を入れて下さい。

1. A coward is incapable of exhibiting love; it (　　　　　)[1] the prerogative of the

   brave.

2. A man (　　　　)[2] but the product of his thoughts.　What (　　　)[3]

   thinks, he becomes.

3. An eye for eye (　　　　)[4] ends up making the whole world blind.

4. Find purpose, the means (　　　　)[5] follow.

5. First they ignore you, then they laugh at (　　　　)[6], then they fight you, then

   you (　　　)[7].

6. Freedom is not worth having if it does (　　　　)[8] include the freedom to

   make mistakes.

7. Happiness is when (　　　　)[9] you think, what you say, and (　　　　)[10]

   you do are in harmony.

8. Hate (　　　)[11] sin, love the sinner.

9. Honest differences are often a healthy (　　　)[12] of progress.

10. I am prepared to die, (　　　　)[13] there is no cause for which I am prepared

    (　　　)[14] kill.

11. In matters of conscience, the law (　　　　)[15] the majority has no place.

12. It is unwise (   )¹⁶ be too sure of one's own wisdom. (   )¹⁷

is healthy to be reminded that the strongest might weaken (   )¹⁸ the

wisest might err.

13. Live as if (   )¹⁹ were to die tomorrow. Learn as if (   )²⁰

were to live forever.

14. Man lives freely only (   )²¹ his readiness to die.

15. Non-violence is the greatest force (   )²² the disposal of mankind. It is

mightier than (   )²³ mightiest weapon of destruction devised by the

ingenuity of man.

16. Strength (   )²⁴ not come from physical capacity. It comes from

(   )²⁵ indomitable will.

17. The future depends on what we (   )²⁶ in the present.

18. The weak can never forgive. Forgiveness (   )²⁷ the attribute of the

strong.

19. There is more (   )²⁸ life than increasing its speed.

20. There is no (   )²⁹ to peace. Peace is the path.

21. To believe (   )³⁰ something and not to live it (   )³¹ dishonest.

22. You must be the change you (   )³² to see in the world.

6 政治家（1）

23. You （   )³³ not lose faith in humanity. Humanity is an ocean; （   )³⁴ a few drops of the ocean are dirty, （   )³⁵ ocean does not become dirty.

24. A slip of （   )³⁶ foot you may soon recover, but （   )³⁷ slip of the tongue you may never （   )³⁸ over.

25. An investment in knowledge always pays the （   )³⁹ interest.

26. Avoid extremes; forbear resenting injuries so much as you think they deserve.

27. Early （   )⁴⁰ bed and early to rise makes a （   )⁴¹ healthy, wealthy, and wise.

28. Genius without education is like silver in （   )⁴² mine.

29. God heals, and the doctor takes the fee.

30. Having （   )⁴³ poor is no shame, but being ashamed of （   )⁴⁴, is.

31. He that is good （   )⁴⁵ making excuses is seldom good for anything else.

32. If （   )⁴⁶ would be loved, love and be lovable.

33. If （   )⁴⁷ would not be forgotten as soon as （   )⁴⁸ are dead, either write things worth reading or do things worth writing.

34. It （   )⁴⁹ a great confidence in a friend to tell （   )⁵⁰ your faults; greater to tell him his.

35. (   )^{51} all your things have their places; let each (   )^{52} of your business have its time.

36. (   )^{53} no time; be always employ'd in something useful; cut (   )^{54} all unnecessary actions.

37. Make no expense but to (   )^{55} good to others or yourself; i.e., waste nothing.

38. Never leave that till tomorrow which (   )^{56} can do today.

39. One today is worth two tomorrow.

40. Resolve to perform what (   )^{57} ought; perform without fail what you resolve.

41. Speak not but (   )^{58} may benefit others or yourself; avoid trifling conversation.

42. Success has ruined many a (   )^{59}.

43. The Constitution only gives people the right to pursue happiness. You (   )^{60} to catch it yourself.

44. The discontented man finds no (   )^{61} chair.

45. The heart of a fool is (   )^{62} his mouth, but the mouth of a (   )^{63} man is in his heart.

6 政治家 (1) 日本語訳

問題英文の日本語訳を確認しよう。

1. 臆病者は愛を表明することができない。それは勇敢さの現れだから。

2. 人は自分の思考の産物にすぎない。したがって，人は自分が思っているものになる。

3. 「目には目を」という考え方は，結果的に，世界中を盲目にしてしまう。

4. 目的を見つけよ。そうすれば，手段は後からついてくる。

5. はじめに彼らはあなたを無視し，次にあなたを笑い，そしてあなたに挑みかかる。そして，最終的に，我々が勝つ。

6. 自由は，持つ価値がない。もし，過ちを犯す自由がないなら。

7. 幸福とは，考えること，言うこと，することがすべて調和している状態だ。

8. 罪を憎み，罪人を愛せ。

9. 率直な意志の相違は，しばしば，進歩の健全な兆候だ。

10. 私には死ぬ覚悟がある。しかし，人を殺す覚悟をさせる理由はどこにもない。

11. 良心の問題に関しては，多数決の法則は当てはまらない。

12. 人間の英知を信用しすぎるのは賢明ではない。次のことを心に留めておくことは健全だ。強者も弱くなるかもしれないし，賢者も間違うかもしれないということだ。

13. 生きよ。明日死ぬかのように。学べ。永遠に生きるかのように。

14. 人は自由に生きられる。死ぬ覚悟ができていれば。

15. 非暴力は人間に与えられた最大の武器だ。人間が発明した最強の破壊兵器より強い。

16. 強さとは，身体能力から来るものではない。不屈の精神から生まれるものだ。

17. 未来は，「今」我々が何を為すかにかかっている。

18. 弱者ほど相手を許すことができない。許しは，強者の性質だ。

19. 人生には，速度を上げる以外に，やることがある。

20. 平和への道はない。平和こそが道なのだ。

21. 何か信じるものがあるのに，それに従って生きないのは，不誠実だ。

22. あなた自身がそうなりなさい。あなたがこの世で見たいと願う変化に。

23. 人間性への信頼を失ってはならない。人間性とは大海に似ている。少し汚れても，海全体が汚れるわけではない。

24. 足を滑らせてもすぐに回復できるかもしれないが，口を滑らせたら，決して乗り越えられないかもしれない。

25. 知識に投資すると，常に最大の利益が得られる。

26. 極端を避けよ。憤慨させるような違法行為にも耐えよ。文字通り，そうであると思っても。

27. 早寝早起きを続ければ，健康，富裕，賢明になる。

28. 教育のない天才は，鉱山に埋もれた銀に似ている。

29. 神が癒し，医者が金を取る。

30. 貧乏であることは恥ではないが，貧乏を恥じていることは，恥だ。

31. 言い訳が上手い人間は，めったに，他に得意なものがない。

32. 愛されたければ，愛し，愛らしくあれ。

33. 死んですぐ忘れられたくなかったら，読むに値する物を書くか，書かれるに値することをせよ。

34. 友人を大いに信頼していれば，自分の失敗を友人に告げる。友人をさらに信頼していれば，友人の失敗を友人に告げる。

35. 物はすべて所を定めて置け。仕事はすべて時を定めてなせ。

36. 一秒も無駄にするな。つねに何か役に立つことに関われ。不必要な行動はするな。

37. 自他に利益がないことに出費するな。つまり，何も浪費するな。

38. 今日できることを明日まで延ばすな。

39. 今日という一日は，明日という日の二日分の価値がある。

40. 実行すべきことを実行するよう決心せよ。決心したことは，必ず実行せよ。

41. 自他に利益があることだけを語れ。取るに足りない会話はするな。

42. 成功によって，多くの人がだめになってきた。

43. 憲法が与えてくれるのは幸福を追求する権利にすぎない。幸福は自分の力でつかまなくてはならない。

44. いつも不満を持っている人は，簡単にはうまくいかない。

45. 愚者の心は口にあるが，賢者の口は心にある。

6 政治家（1）解答

1. A coward is incapable of exhibiting love; it (**is**)[1] the prerogative of the brave.

2. A man (**is**)[2] but the product of his thoughts.   What (**he**)[3] thinks, he becomes.

3. An eye for eye (**only**)[4] ends up making the whole world blind.

4. Find purpose, the means (**will**)[5] follow.

5. First they ignore you, then they laugh at (**you**)[6], then they fight you, then you (**win**)[7].

6. Freedom is not worth having if it does (**not**)[8] include the freedom to make mistakes.

7. Happiness is when (**what**)[9] you think, what you say, and (**what**)[10] you do are in harmony.

8. Hate (**the**)[11] sin, love the sinner.

9. Honest differences are often a healthy (**sign**)[12] of progress.

10. I am prepared to die, (**but**)[13] there is no cause for which I am prepared (**to**)[14] kill.

11. In matters of conscience, the law (**of**)[15] the majority has no place.

12. It is unwise (**to**)[16] be too sure of one's own wisdom.   (**It**)[17] is healthy to be reminded that the strongest might weaken (**and**)[18] the wisest might err.

13. Live as if (**you**)[19] were to die tomorrow.   Learn as if (**you**)[20] were to live forever.

14. Man lives freely only (**by**)[21] his readiness to die.

15. Non-violence is the greatest force (**at**)[22] the disposal of mankind.   It is mightier than (**the**)[23] mightiest weapon of destruction devised by the ingenuity of man.

16. Strength (**does**)[24] not come from physical capacity.   It comes from (**an**)[25] indomitable will.

17. The future depends on what we (**do**)[26] in the present.

18. The weak can never forgive.   Forgiveness (**is**)[27] the attribute of the strong.

19. There is more (**to**)[28] life than increasing its speed.

20. There is no (**path**)[29] to peace.   Peace is the path.

21. To believe (**in**)[30] something and not to live it (**is**)[31] dishonest.

22. You must be the change you (**want**)[32] to see in the world.

23. You (**must**)[33] not lose faith in humanity.   Humanity is an ocean; (**if**)[34] a few drops of the ocean are dirty, (**the**)[35] ocean does not become dirty.

24. A slip of (**the**)[36] foot you may soon recover, but (**a**)[37] slip of the tongue you may never (**get**)[38] over.

25. An investment in knowledge always pays the (**best**)[39] interest.

26. Avoid extremes; forbear resenting injuries so much as you think they deserve.

27. Early (**to**)[40] bed and early to rise makes a (**man**)[41] healthy, wealthy, and wise.

28. Genius without education is like silver in (**the**)^{42} mine.

29. God heals, and the doctor takes the fee.

30. Having (**been**)^{43} poor is no shame, but being ashamed of (**it**)^{44}, is.

31. He that is good (**for**)^{45} making excuses is seldom good for anything else.

32. If (**you**)^{46} would be loved, love and be lovable.

33. If (**you**)^{47} would not be forgotten as soon as (**you**)^{48} are dead, either write things worth reading or do things worth writing.

34. It (**is**)^{49} a great confidence in a friend to tell (**him**)^{50} your faults; greater to tell him his.

35. (**Let**)^{51} all your things have their places; let each (**part**)^{52} of your business have its time.

36. (**Lose**)^{53} no time; be always employ'd in something useful; cut (**off**)^{54} all unnecessary actions.

37. Make no expense but to (**do**)^{55} good to others or yourself; i.e., waste nothing.

38. Never leave that till tomorrow which (**you**)^{56} can do today.

39. One today is worth two tomorrow.

40. Resolve to perform what (**you**)^{57} ought; perform without fail what you resolve.

41. Speak not but (**what**)^{58} may benefit others or yourself; avoid trifling conversation.

42. Success has ruined many a (**man**)^{59}.

43. The Constitution only gives people the right to pursue happiness. You (**have**)^{60} to catch it yourself.

44. The discontented man finds no (**easy**)^{61} chair.

45. The heart of a fool is (**in**)^{62} his mouth, but the mouth of a (**wise**)^{63} man is in his heart.

7 教育家・活動家 (1)

CD を聞きながら，（ 　　　　　）の中に，4文字以下の英単語を入れて下さい。

1. How very little can be done under (　　　　)[1] spirit of fear.

2. I attribute my success to (　　　　)[2]—I never gave or took any excuse.

3. (　　　　)[3] never lose an opportunity of urging a practical beginning, however small, for (　　　)[4] is wonderful how often in such matters the mustard-seed germinates (　　　　)[5] roots itself.

4. I stand at the altar of the murdered (　　　　)[6], and, while I live, I fight their cause.

5. The (　　　)[7] first requirement in a hospital is that it should (　　　　)[8] the sick no harm.

6. Do (　　　)[9] you feel in your heart to (　　　)[10] right—for you'll be criticized anyway.

7. The future belongs to those who believe (　　　　)[11] the beauty of their dreams.

8. Life was meant to (　　　)[12] lived, and curiosity must be kept alive. One must never, (　　　)[13] whatever reason, turn his back on life.

9. (　　　)[14] woman is like a tea bag; (　　　)[15] never know how strong it is until it's in (　　　)[16] water.

10. Beautiful young people are accidents of nature, but beautiful old people are works (　　　)[17] art.

11. One's philosophy is not best expressed in words; (　　　)[18] is expressed in the choices one makes ... and the choices (　　　)[19] make are ultimately our responsibility.

12. It is better ( )^{20} light a single candle than to curse the darkness.

13. It ( )^{21} not fair to ask of others ( )^{22} you are unwilling to do yourself.

14. Never mistake knowledge for wisdom. One helps ( )^{23} make a living; the other helps you make ( )^{24} life.

15. Learn from the mistakes of others. You can't ( )^{25} long enough to make them all yourself.

16. Great minds discuss ideas; Average minds discuss events; Small minds discuss people.

17. ( )^{26} one thing everyday that scares you.

18. To handle yourself, use your ( )^{27}; to handle others, use your heart.

19. If someone betrays you ( )^{28}, it's their fault; if they betray you twice, it's your fault.

20. People grow through experience ( )^{29} they meet life honestly and courageously. This ( )^{30} how character is built.

21. Character building begins in our infancy and continues until death.

22. One thing ( )^{31} has taught me: If you are interested, ( )^{32} never have to look for new interests. ( )^{33} come to you. When you ( )^{34} genuinely interested in one thing, it will always lead to something ( )^{35}.

23. No one can make you feel inferior without ( )^{36} consent.

24. I can not believe that war ( )^{37} the best solution. No one won the ( )^{38} war, and no one will win ( )^{39} next war.

25. Keep your face ( )^{40} the sunshine and you cannot see the shadow.

7 教育家・活動家 (1)

26. (   )^41 can do anything we want to (   )^42 we stick to it long

    enough.

27. Never bend (   )^43 head. Always hold it high. Look (   )^44

    world straight in the eye.

28. Be of (   )^45 cheer. Do not think of today's failures, but of

    (   )^46 success that may come tomorrow.

29. We could never learn to (   )^47 brave and patient, if there were only joy

    (   )^48 the world.

30. Face your deficiencies and acknowledge them; (   )^49 do not let them

    master you. (   )^50 them teach you patience, sweetness, insight.

31. When we do (   )^51 best that we can, we never (   )^52 what

    miracle is wrought in our life, (   )^53 in the life of another.

32. When one (   )^54 of happiness closes, another opens; but often we look

    so (   )^55 at the closed door that we (   )^56 not see the one

    which has been opened (   )^57 us.

33. So long as you (   )^58 sweeten another's pain, life is not in

    (   )^59.

34. The most pathetic person in the world is someone (   )^60 has sight, but

    has no vision.

35. I (   )^61 to accomplish a great and noble task, but (   )^62 is my

    chief duty to accomplish small tasks as (   )^63 they were great and

    noble.

36. The best (   )^64 most beautiful things in the world cannot be seen

    (   )^65 even touched. They must be felt (   )^66 the heart.

37. Remember, no effort that we make (　　　　　)^{67} attain something beautiful is ever lost.

38. Joy is (　　　　　)^{68} holy fire that keeps our purpose warm (　　　　　)^{69} our intelligence aglow.

39. Character cannot be developed in ease and quiet. (　　　　　)^{70} through experience of trial and suffering can the soul (　　　　　)^{71} strengthened, vision cleared, ambition inspired, and success achieved.

40. I would rather walk with a friend (　　　　　)^{72} the dark, than alone in the light.

41. (　　　　　)^{73} sympathies are with all who struggle for justice.

42. (　　　　　)^{74} pessimist ever discovered the secret of the stars, or sailed (　　　　　)^{75} an uncharted land, or opened a new doorway (　　　　　)^{76} the human spirit.

43. Security is mostly a superstition. It does (　　　　　)^{77} exist in nature, nor do the children of (　　　　　)^{78} as a whole experience it. Avoiding danger is no safer (　　　　　)^{79} the long run than outright exposure. Life (　　　　　)^{80} either a daring adventure, or nothing.

44. You have set yourselves (　　　　　)^{81} difficult task, but you will succeed if (　　　　　)^{82} persevere; and you will find a (　　　　　)^{83} in overcoming obstacles.

45. Science may have found a cure (　　　　　)^{84} most evils; but it has found no remedy (　　　　　)^{85} the worst of them all—the apathy (　　　　　)^{86} human beings.

7 教育家・活動家（1）日本語訳

問題英文の日本語訳を確認しよう。

1. 恐れを抱いていては，何とものごとが成し遂げられないことか。

2. 私が成功したのは，このためだ。決して言い訳したり，言い訳を受け入れなかったことだ。

3. 物事を始めるチャンスを，私は逃さない。どれだけ小さなチャンスでも。マスタードの種が，芽を出し，根を張るようなことがいくらでもあるからだ。

4. 私は，命を奪われた男たちの祭壇の前に立つ。生きている限り，彼らを死に追いやった相手と戦う。

5. 病院の第一の条件は，患者に害を与えないことだ。

6. あなたが正しいと思うことをせよ。何をしたって批判されるのだから。

7. 未来は，こんな人のためにある。自分が見る夢の美しさを信じる人のために。

8. 人生は，生ききること。好奇心は，持ち続けること。どんな理由があっても，決して人生に背を向けるな。

9. 女性はティーバッグに似ている。人は，その強さに気づかない。熱湯につけられるまでは。

10. 若くて美しいことは，自然のいたずらだ。しかし，年をとっても美しいことは芸術だ。

11. 人の哲学を一番よく表すのは，言葉ではない。それは，その人の選択による。我々の選択とは，結局，我々の責任である。

12. ローソクに灯をともせ。暗闇が不愉快なら。

13. 次のようなことは，フェアではない。自分がやりたくないことを他人に頼むことは。

14. 知識と賢明さを取り違えるな。知識は生計を立てるのに役立つが，賢明さは人生を豊かにするのに役立つ。

15. 他人の失敗から学べ。あなたは人の失敗をすべて経験できるほど長くは生きられない。

16. 偉大な心の持ち主は，アイディアについて話し，凡庸な心の持ち主は，出来事について話し，狭量な心の持ち主は，人々について話す。

17. 毎日，あなたが恐れていることを一つ行え。

18. 自分自身を扱う際には，頭を使え。他人を扱う際には，心を使え。

19. もし誰かが一度あなたを裏切ったら，それは彼らの責任だ。もし彼らが二度あなたを裏切ったら，それはあなたの責任だ。

20. 人間は経験を通じて成長する。正直に勇気を持って人生と向かいあえば。そうやって人格が作られる。

21. 性格の形成は幼児期に始まり，死ぬまで続く。

22. 人生が私に教えてくれたことは，こんなことだ。何かに興味を持っていれば，新しい興味を探す必要はない。向こうからこっちにやってくる。真に一つのことに興味を持てば，必ず違う何かにつながっていく。

23. 誰もあなたに劣等感を抱かせることはできない。あなたの同意なしに。

24. こんなことは，信じられない。戦争が最高の解決策だということは。この前の戦争で勝った者は誰もいなかったし，この次の戦争で勝つ者も誰もいない。

25. 顔をいつも太陽の方に向けていなさい。そうすれば，影なんて見ることはないから。

26. 私たちは，望めば，どんなことだってできる。あきらめずにさえいれば。

27. うつむいてはいけない。いつも頭を高くあげていなさい。世の中をまっすぐ見つめなさい。

28. 元気を出そう。今日の失敗をあれこれ考えず，明日訪れるかもしれない成功について考えよう。

29. 人は決して勇気と忍耐を学ばないだろう。この世に喜びしかなければ。

30. 自分の欠点を直視し，認めよ。ただし欠点に振り回されてはいけない。そこから，忍耐力，優しさ，洞察力を学び取れ。

31. 最善を尽くしてみると，思いがけない奇跡が起こるかもしれない。自分の人生にも，他人の人生にも。

32. 一つの幸せのドアが閉じると，もう一つのドアが開く。しかし，よく私たちは，閉じたドアばかりを見つめ，開いたドアに気付かない。

33. 人の苦しみをやわらげてあげられる限り，生きている価値がある。

34. 世界で最も哀れな人とは，このような人だ。目は見えていても，どうすべきか分からない人だ。

35. 私は，素晴らしく尊い仕事を成し遂げたいが，私の義務は，些細な仕事も，素晴らしく尊い仕事であるかのように，成し遂げることだ。

36. 世界で最も素晴らしく，最も美しいものは，目で見たり手で触れたりすることはできない。それは，心で感じなければならない。

37. 次のことを覚えておきなさい。何か素晴らしいことを達成するために払う努力は，決して無駄にはならないということを。

38. 喜びとは，神聖な炎だ。目的を温め続け，知性を輝かせ続ける炎だ。

39. 性格は安らぎや静けさの中で生まれるものではない。試練や苦しみを経験することによってのみ，魂が鍛えられ，洞察力が研ぎ澄まされ，野心が鼓舞され，成功が得られる。

40. 私は，闇の中を友人と共に歩む方を好む。光の中を一人で歩むよりも。

41. 私は，共感する。正義のために戦っている人すべてに。

42. こんなことは，いまだかつてない。悲観論者が，星の秘密を発見したり，海図にない陸地を求めて航海したり，精神世界に新たな扉を開いたりしたことは。

43. 安全とは，ほとんどの場合，迷信だ。現実には安全は存在せず，子供たちは，誰一人として安全を経験しない。危険を避けるのは，危険に身をさらすのと同じ程度に危険だ。人生は危険に満ちた冒険か，あるいは，何もないか，そのどちらかだ。

44. あなたは困難な仕事を自分に課したが，きっとうまくいくだろう。あきらめずに進めば。そして，喜びすら見出すだろう。成功への障害を克服することに。

45. 科学は，大抵の害悪に対して解決策を見出したかもしれない。しかし，その中の最悪のものに対しては，まったく救済策を見出していない。その最悪のものとは，人間の無関心さだ。

7 教育・活動家 (1) 解答

1. How very little can be done under (**the**)[1] spirit of fear.

2. I attribute my success to (**this**)[2]—I never gave or took any excuse.

3. (**I**)[3] never lose an opportunity of urging a practical beginning, however small, for (**it**)[4] is wonderful how often in such matters the mustard-seed germinates (**and**)[5] roots itself.

4. I stand at the altar of the murdered (**men**)[6], and, while I live, I fight their cause.

5. The (**very**)[7] first requirement in a hospital is that it should (**do**)[8] the sick no harm.

6. Do (**what**)[9] you feel in your heart to (**be**)[10] right—for you'll be criticized anyway.

7. The future belongs to those who believe (**in**)[11] the beauty of their dreams.

8. Life was meant to (**be**)[12] lived, and curiosity must be kept alive. One must never, (**for**)[13] whatever reason, turn his back on life.

9. (**A**)[14] woman is like a tea bag; (**you**)[15] never know how strong it is until it's in (**hot**)[16] water.

10. Beautiful young people are accidents of nature, but beautiful old people are works (**of**)[17] art.

11. One's philosophy is not best expressed in words; (**it**)[18] is expressed in the choices one makes … and the choices (**we**)[19] make are ultimately our responsibility.

12. It is better (**to**)[20] light a single candle than to curse the darkness.

13. It (**is**)[21] not fair to ask of others (**what**)[22] you are unwilling to do yourself.

14. Never mistake knowledge for wisdom. One helps (**you**)[23] make a living; the other helps you make (**a**)[24] life.

15. Learn from the mistakes of others. You can't (**live**)[25] long enough to make them all yourself.

16. Great minds discuss ideas; Average minds discuss events; Small minds discuss people.

17. (**Do**)[26] one thing everyday that scares you.

18. To handle yourself, use your (**head**)[27]; to handle others, use your heart.

19. If someone betrays you (**once**)[28], it's their fault; if they betray you twice, it's your fault.

20. People grow through experience (**if**)[29] they meet life honestly and courageously. This (**is**)[30] how character is built.

21. Character building begins in our infancy and continues until death.

22. One thing (**life**)[31] has taught me: If you are interested, (**you**)[32] never have to look for new interests. (**They**)[33] come to you. When you (**are**)[34] genuinely interested in one thing, it will always lead to something (**else**)[35].

23. No one can make you feel inferior without (**your**)[36] consent.

24. I can not believe that war (**is**)[37] the best solution. No one won the (**last**)[38] war, and no one will win (**the**)[39] next war.

25. Keep your face (**to**)[40] the sunshine and you cannot see the shadow.

26. (**We**)^{41} can do anything we want to (**if**)^{42} we stick to it long enough.

27. Never bend (**your**)^{43} head.　Always hold it high.　Look (**the**)^{44} world straight in the eye.

28. Be of (**good**)^{45} cheer.　Do not think of today's failures, but of (**the**)^{46} success that may come tomorrow.

29. We could never learn to (**be**)^{47} brave and patient, if there were only joy (**in**)^{48} the world.

30. Face your deficiencies and acknowledge them; (**but**)^{49} do not let them master you.　(**Let**)^{50} them teach you patience, sweetness, insight.

31. When we do (**the**)^{51} best that we can, we never (**know**)^{52} what miracle is wrought in our life, (**or**)^{53} in the life of another.

32. When one (**door**)^{54} of happiness closes, another opens; but often we look so (**long**)^{55} at the closed door that we (**do**)^{56} not see the one which has been opened (**for**)^{57} us.

33. So long as you (**can**)^{58} sweeten another's pain, life is not in (**vain**)^{59}.

34. The most pathetic person in the world is someone (**who**)^{60} has sight, but has no vision.

35. I (**long**)^{61} to accomplish a great and noble task, but (**it**)^{62} is my chief duty to accomplish small tasks as (**if**)^{63} they were great and noble.

36. The best (**and**)^{64} most beautiful things in the world cannot be seen (**or**)^{65} even touched. They must be felt (**with**)^{66} the heart.

37. Remember, no effort that we make (**to**)^{67} attain something beautiful is ever lost.

38. Joy is (**the**)^{68} holy fire that keeps our purpose warm (**and**)^{69} our intelligence aglow.

39. Character cannot be developed in ease and quiet.　(**Only**)^{70} through experience of trial and suffering can the soul (**be**)^{71} strengthened, vision cleared, ambition inspired, and success achieved.

40. I would rather walk with a friend (**in**)^{72} the dark, than alone in the light.

41. (**My**)^{73} sympathies are with all who struggle for justice.

42. (**No**)^{74} pessimist ever discovered the secret of the stars, or sailed (**to**)^{75} an uncharted land, or opened a new doorway (**for**)^{76} the human spirit.

43. Security is mostly a superstition.　It does (**not**)^{77} exist in nature, nor do the children of (**men**)^{78} as a whole experience it.　Avoiding danger is no safer (**in**)^{79} the long run than outright exposure.　Life (**is**)^{80} either a daring adventure, or nothing.

44. You have set yourselves (**a**)^{81} difficult task, but you will succeed if (**you**)^{82} persevere; and you will find a (**joy**)^{83} in overcoming obstacles.

45. Science may have found a cure (**for**)^{84} most evils; but it has found no remedy (**for**)^{85} the worst of them all—the apathy (**of**)^{86} human beings.

8 科学者 (2)

1–9 Galileo Galilei/ガリレオ・ガリレイ (1564年〜1642年)
10–32 Blaise Pascal/ブレーズ・パスカル (1623年〜1662年)
33–45 Isaac Newton/アイザック・ニュートン (1642年〜1727年)

CDを聞きながら，（ 　　　　　　　）の中に，4文字以下の英単語を入れて下さい。

1. I've loved the stars too fondly to be fearful of (　　　　　)^1 night.

2. Mathematics is the alphabet with which God has written the Universe.

3. Mathematics (　　　　　)^2 the key and door to (　　　　　)^3 sciences.

4. Names and attributes must be accommodated to the essence (　　　　　)^4 things, and not the essence to the names, since things (　　　　　)^5 first and names afterwards.

5. Philosophy is written in that great book which (　　　　　)^6 lies before our eyes —I mean (　　　　　)^7 universe.

6. The Bible shows the way to go (　　　　　)^8 heaven, not the way the heavens go.

7. (　　　　　)^9 book is written in the mathematical language, and (　　　　　)^{10} symbols are triangles, circles and other geometrical figures, without whose help it is impossible (　　　　　)^{11} comprehend a single word of it; without which one wanders in (　　　　　)^{12} through a dark labyrinth.

8. Where the senses fail us, reason (　　　　　)^{13} step in.

9. You cannot teach a man anything, (　　　　　)^{14} can only help him find (　　　　　)^{15} within himself.

10. All human evil comes from a single cause, man's inability to (   )^{16} still

in a room.

11. Curiosity is only vanity. (   )^{17} usually only want to know something

so (   )^{18} we can talk about it.

12. Few friendships would survive (   )^{19} each one knew what his friend

says (   )^{20} him behind his back.

13. If all (   )^{21} knew what others say of them, there would (   )^{22}

be four friends in the world.

14. If Cleopatra's nose (   )^{23} been shorter, the whole face of the earth

would (   )^{24} changed.

15. If you want people to think well (   )^{25} you, do not speak well of your-

self.

16. Imagination disposes (   )^{26} everything; it creates beauty, justice, and

happiness, which are everything in this world.

17. (   )^{27} is incomprehensible that God should exist, and it is incomprehen-

sible (   )^{28} he should not exist.

18. Justice without force is powerless; force without justice is tyrannical.

19. Kind words (   )^{29} not cost much.   Yet they accomplish (   )^{30}.

20. Little things console us because little things afflict us.

21. Man is but (   )^{31} reed, the most feeble thing in nature, but

(   )^{32} is a thinking reed.

8 科学者 (2)

22. Man is (   )³³ a disguise, a liar, a hypocrite, both (   )³⁴ himself and to others.

23. Man's greatness lies in his power (   )³⁵ thought.

24. Noble deeds that are concealed are most esteemed.

25. The eternal silence (   )³⁶ these infinite spaces frightens me.

26. The heart has its reasons of which reason knows nothing.

27. (   )³⁷ strength of a man's virtue should not be measured by (   )³⁸ special exertions, but by his habitual acts.

28. There are (   )³⁹ two kinds of men: the righteous who think they (   )⁴⁰ sinners and the sinners who think they are righteous.

29. (   )⁴¹ heals griefs and quarrels, for we change and are (   )⁴² longer the same persons.   Neither the offender nor the offended (   )⁴³ any more themselves.

30. To make light of philosophy (   )⁴⁴ to be a true philosopher.

31. We (   )⁴⁵ the truth, not only by the reason, (   )⁴⁶ also by the heart.

32. We never, then, (   )⁴⁷ a person, but only qualities.

33. A man (   )⁴⁸ imagine things that are false, but he can (   )⁴⁹ understand things that are true, for if (   )⁵⁰ things be false, the apprehension of them is (   )⁵¹ understanding.

34. God created everything by number, weight and measure.

35. I can calculate the motion (   )^{52} heavenly bodies but not the madness of people.

36. I frame (   )^{53} hypotheses.

37. I was like a boy playing (   )^{54} the sea-shore, and diverting myself now and then finding (   )^{55} smoother pebble or a prettier shell than ordinary, whilst the great ocean of truth (   )^{56} all undiscovered before me.

38. If I have (   )^{57} made any valuable discoveries, it has been owing (   )^{58} to patient attention, than to any other talent.

39. If (   )^{59} have seen further, it is by standing (   )^{60} the shoulders of giants.

40. Men build too many walls (   )^{61} not enough bridges.

41. Plato is my friend, Aristotle is my friend, (   )^{62} my best friend is truth.

42. Tact is (   )^{63} knack of making a point without making an enemy.

43. This most beautiful system (   )^{64} the sun, planets, and comets, could only proceed from (   )^{65} counsel and dominion of an intelligent and powerful Being.

44. To every action there (   )^{66} always opposed an equal reaction.

45. Truth is ever to be found (   )^{67} simplicity, and not in the multiplicity and confusion (   )^{68} things.

8　科学者（2）日本語訳

問題英文の日本語訳を確認しよう。

1. 私はあまりにも深く星を愛してきたので，夜を恐れなくなった。

2. 数学は，アルファベットだ。神が宇宙を書いた。

3. 数学は，鍵とドアだ。諸科学へとつながる。

4. 名前や属性は，物事の本質に一致すべきで，本質を名前に合わせるべきではない。最初に事物が存在し，名前はその後に続くものだからだ。

5. 哲学は，この巨大な書物に書かれている。我々の目の前に広がる，「宇宙」という書物に。

6. 聖書は我々がいかに天へ行くかを教える。いかに天体が動くかを教えてはくれない。

7. この「宇宙」という書物は，数学という言語で書かれている。そしてその文字は，三角形，円，そして，その他の幾何学図形だ。これがなければ，この書物の言葉は人間には一つも理解できない。これがなければ，人は暗い迷路をたださまようばかりだ。

8. 感覚が役に立たない時，理性が役に立ち始めるにちがいない。

9. 人にものを教えることはできない。自分自身の中に気づかせる手助けができるだけだ。

10. 人間の悪事はすべて，たった一つの原因に由来する。それは，部屋の中でじっとしていられないということだ。

11. 好奇心は，虚栄心にすぎない。大抵の場合，何かを知りたがる人は，それについて人に話したいだけだ。

12. 友情など，ほとんど，存在しない。自分の友人が陰でしゃべっていることをお互いに知ったなら。

13. すべての人が，互いについて何を話しているか知ったなら，この世に友は4人といないだろう。

14. クレオパトラの鼻がもう少し低かったら，世界の歴史は変わっていただろう。

15. 人によく思われたいなら，自分を褒めないことだ。

16. 想像力は，何でもやる。それは，美と正義と幸福を作り出す。これが，この世におけるすべてだ。

17. 神が存在するということは不可解で，神が存在しないということも不可解だ。

18. 力なき正義は無力だ。正義なき力は圧制だ。

19. 親切な言葉を口に出しても，金はかからない。しかし，多くを成し遂げてくれる。

20. 些細なことが私たちの慰めになる。それは，些細なことが私たちの苦しみになるからだ。

21. 人間は，一本の葦にすぎない。自然のうちで最も弱いものだ。しかし，それは考える葦だ。

22. 人間は，偽装と虚偽と偽善にほかならない。自分自身に対しても，また他人に対しても。

23. 人間の偉大さは，考える力にある。

24. 高潔な行いは，隠れてなされれば，最も尊敬される。

25. この無限空間の永遠の静けさに，私は，ぞっとする。

26. 心には，理性では分からない理由がある。

27. 人間の徳の高さは，その人間の特別な行動で判断されるべきではない。日頃の行いで判断されるべきだ。

28. 人間には二種類しかいない。自分を罪人だと思っている善人と，自分を善人だと思っている罪人だ。

29. 時は，悲しみと口論の傷を癒してくれる。人はみな変わり，過去の自分はもはや現在の自分ではないからだ。攻撃する者も攻撃される者も，時が経てば別人になる。

30. 哲学を嘲笑することこそ，真の哲学者であることだ。

31. 我々は，真理を知る。理性によってのみではなく，心によっても。

32. 我々が本当に愛するのは，人間そのものではなくて，人間が持っている特性だ。

33. 人間は，事実に反することを想像してもよいが，真実であることしか理解できない。そのことが誤っていたら，それが分かった気になっていることは，理解ではないからだ。

34. 神は，すべてを創造した。数と重さと尺度によって。

35. 天体の動きは計算できるが，群集の狂気は計算できない。

36. 私は，いかなる仮説も立てない。

37. 私は，海辺で遊んでいる少年のようだった。たまに，普通のものよりなめらかな小石やかわいい貝殻を見つけて夢中になっていた。真理の大海は，すべてが未発見のまま，目の前に広がっていたのに。

38. 私が価値ある発見をしたとすれば，それは，忍耐強く注意を払っていたことによるものだ。他の才能ではまったくなく。

39. 私が遠くを見ることができたとすれば，巨人たちの肩に乗っていたからだ。

40. 人はあまりにも多くの壁を造るが，架け橋の数は十分ではない。

41. プラトンは私の友，アリストテレスは私の友だ。しかし，私の最大の友は真理だ。

42. 如才なさとは，自分を主張する技だ。敵を作らずに。

43. 太陽，惑星，彗星からなる最も美しい系は，知性と力ある存在の配慮と支配からのみ発生しえた。

44. どんな行動にも，必ずそれと等しい反対の反応がある。

45. 真理は，つねに単純さの中に見出される。事物の多様さと混乱のうちにではなく。

8 科学者 (2) 解答

1. I've loved the stars too fondly to be fearful of (**the**)[1] night.

2. Mathematics is the alphabet with which God has written the Universe.

3. Mathematics (**is**)[2] the key and door to (**the**)[3] sciences.

4. Names and attributes must be accommodated to the essence (**of**)[4] things, and not the essence to the names, since things (**come**)[5] first and names afterwards.

5. Philosophy is written in that great book which (**ever**)[6] lies before our eyes—I mean (**the**)[7] universe.

6. The Bible shows the way to go (**to**)[8] heaven, not the way the heavens go.

7. (**This**)[9] book is written in the mathematical language, and (**the**)[10] symbols are triangles, circles and other geometrical figures, without whose help it is impossible (**to**)[11] comprehend a single word of it; without which one wanders in (**vain**)[12] through a dark labyrinth.

8. Where the senses fail us, reason (**must**)[13] step in.

9. You cannot teach a man anything, (**you**)[14] can only help him find (**it**)[15] within himself.

10. All human evil comes from a single cause, man's inability to (**sit**)[16] still in a room.

11. Curiosity is only vanity.　(**We**)[17] usually only want to know something so (**that**)[18] we can talk about it.

12. Few friendships would survive (**if**)[19] each one knew what his friend says (**of**)[20] him behind his back.

13. If all (**men**)[21] knew what others say of them, there would (**not**)[22] be four friends in the world.

14. If Cleopatra's nose (**had**)[23] been shorter, the whole face of the earth would (**have**)[24] changed.

15. If you want people to think well (**of**)[25] you, do not speak well of yourself.

16. Imagination disposes (**of**)[26] everything; it creates beauty, justice, and happiness, which are everything in this world.

17. (**It**)[27] is incomprehensible that God should exist, and it is incomprehensible (**that**)[28] he should not exist.

18. Justice without force is powerless; force without justice is tyrannical.

19. Kind words (**do**)[29] not cost much.　Yet they accomplish (**much**)[30].

20. Little things console us because little things afflict us.

21. Man is but (**a**)[31] reed, the most feeble thing in nature, but (**he**)[32] is a thinking reed.

22. Man is (**only**)[33] a disguise, a liar, a hypocrite, both (**to**)[34] himself and to others.

23. Man's greatness lies in his power (**of**)[35] thought.

24. Noble deeds that are concealed are most esteemed.

25. The eternal silence (**of**)[36] these infinite spaces frightens me.

26. The heart has its reasons of which reason knows nothing.

27. (**The**)[37] strength of a man's virtue should not be measured by (**his**)[38] special exertions, but by his habitual acts.

28. There are (**only**)[39] two kinds of men: the righteous who think they (**are**)[40] sinners and the sinners who think they are righteous.

29. (**Time**)[41] heals griefs and quarrels, for we change and are (**no**)[42] longer the same persons. Neither the offender nor the offended (**are**)[43] any more themselves.

30. To make light of philosophy (**is**)[44] to be a true philosopher.

31. We (**know**)[45] the truth, not only by the reason, (**but**)[46] also by the heart.

32. We never, then, (**love**)[47] a person, but only qualities.

33. A man (**may**)[48] imagine things that are false, but he can (**only**)[49] understand things that are true, for if (**the**)[50] things be false, the apprehension of them is (**not**)[51] understanding.

34. God created everything by number, weight and measure.

35. I can calculate the motion (**of**)[52] heavenly bodies but not the madness of people.

36. I frame (**no**)[53] hypotheses.

37. I was like a boy playing (**on**)[54] the sea-shore, and diverting myself now and then finding (**a**)[55] smoother pebble or a prettier shell than ordinary, whilst the great ocean of truth (**lay**)[56] all undiscovered before me.

38. If I have (**ever**)[57] made any valuable discoveries, it has been owing (**more**)[58] to patient attention, than to any other talent.

39. If (**I**)[59] have seen further, it is by standing (**on**)[60] the shoulders of giants.

40. Men build too many walls (**and**)[61] not enough bridges.

41. Plato is my friend, Aristotle is my friend, (**but**)[62] my best friend is truth.

42. Tact is (**the**)[63] knack of making a point without making an enemy.

43. This most beautiful system (**of**)[64] the sun, planets, and comets, could only proceed from (**the**)[65] counsel and dominion of an intelligent and powerful Being.

44. To every action there (**is**)[66] always opposed an equal reaction.

45. Truth is ever to be found (**in**)[67] simplicity, and not in the multiplicity and confusion (**of**)[68] things.

9　哲学者 (2)

1-26 Aristotle/アリストテレス (紀元前 384 年〜前 322 年)
27-45 René Descartes/ルネ・デカルト (1596 年〜1650 年)

CD を聞きながら, (　　　　　　　) の中に, 4 文字以下の英単語を入れて下さい。

1. Happiness depends upon ourselves.

2. Happiness is the meaning and the purpose (　　　　　　)[1] life, the whole aim and end of human existence.

3. (　　　　　)[2] who is to be a (　　　　　)[3] ruler must have first been ruled.

4. Hope is (　　　　　)[4] waking dream.

5. I count him braver who overcomes his desires (　　　　　)[5] him who conquers his enemies; for the hardest victory (　　　　　)[6] over self.

6. It is the (　　　　　)[7] of an educated mind to be (　　　　　)[8] to entertain a thought without accepting it.

7. Love is composed (　　　　　)[9] a single soul inhabiting two bodies.

8. Man is a (　　　　　)[10] seeking animal. His life only has meaning if (　　　　　)[11] is reaching out and striving for his goals.

9. Misfortune shows those (　　　　　)[12] are not really friends.

10. Mothers are fonder than fathers of their children because (　　　　　)[13] are more certain they are their own.

11. Nature (　　　　　)[14] nothing uselessly.

12. Pleasure in the job puts perfection in (　　　　　)[15] work.

13. Revolutions are not about trifles, but spring from trifles.

14. Shame (   )^{16} an ornament to the young; a disgrace to (   )^{17}

old.

15. The aim of art (   )^{18} to represent not the outward appearance of things,

but their inward significance.

16. (   )^{19} greatest virtues are those which are most useful to other persons.

17. The (   )^{20} stable state is the one in which all men (   )^{21} equal

before the law.

18. The roots of education are bitter, (   )^{22} the fruit is sweet.

19. Those that know, do.   Those (   )^{23} understand, teach.

20. Time crumbles things; everything grows old under the power of Time

(   )^{24} is forgotten through the lapse of Time.

21. To (   )^{25} conscious that we are perceiving or thinking is (   )^{26}

be conscious of our own existence.

22. To perceive (   )^{27} to suffer.

23. We are what we repeatedly (   )^{28}.   Excellence, then, is not an act,

(   )^{29} a habit.

24. Well begun is half done.

25. Without friends (   )^{30} one would choose to live, though he had all other

goods.

26. Youth (   )^{31} easily deceived because it is quick to hope.

9 哲学者 (2)

27. An optimist ( )^{32} see a light where there is none, but ( )^{33}

    must the pessimist always run to blow ( )^{34} out?

28. Conquer yourself rather than the world.

29. Divide each difficulty into ( )^{35} many parts as is feasible and necessary

    to resolve ( )^{36}.

30. Doubt is the origin of wisdom.

31. Everything is self-evident.

32. Except our ( )^{37} thoughts, there is nothing absolutely in our power.

33. For nothing causes regret and remorse except irresolution.

34. ( )^{38} sense is of all things in the world ( )^{39} most equally

    distributed.

35. I think, therefore I am.

36. If ( )^{40} would be a real seeker after truth, it is necessary

    ( )^{41} at least once in your life ( )^{42} doubt, as far as possible,

    all things.

37. Illusory joy ( )^{43} often worth more than genuine sorrow.

38. In order to improve the ( )^{44}, we ought less to learn, than to contem-

    plate.

39. ( )^{45} is not enough to have a ( )^{46} mind. The main thing is

    to ( )^{47} it well.

40. Perfect numbers like perfect men are (   )[48] rare.

41. The chief cause of human errors is to (   )[49] found in the prejudices picked up in childhood.

42. The greatest minds (   )[50] capable of the greatest vices as well as (   )[51] the greatest virtues.

43. The reading of all good books (   )[52] like a conversation with the finest minds of (   )[53] centuries.

44. To know what people really think, pay regard to (   )[54] they do, rather than what they (   )[55].

45. Whenever anyone has offended me, I try to raise (   )[56] soul so high that the offense cannot reach (   )[57].

9 哲学者 (2) 日本語訳

問題英文の日本語訳を確認しよう。

1. 幸せかどうかは，自分次第だ。

2. 幸福は，人生の意味および目標で，人間の存在の究極の目的および狙いだ。

3. 良き指導者は，まず，人に従ったことがなければならない。

4. 希望とは，目覚めていて抱く夢だ。

5. 私は，このような者を勇者と見る。敵を倒した者より，自分の欲望を克服した者の方だ。最も難しい勝利は，自らに勝つことだからだ。

6. これは，教育された精神の証だ。ある思想を受け入れずに，それを楽しめることは。

7. 愛は，二つの肉体に宿る一つの魂からなっている。

8. 人間は，目標を追い求める動物だ。その人生が意味あるものとなるのは，目標へ到達しようと努力していることによってのみだ。

9. 不幸によって，本当の友人でない者が明らかになる。

10. 母親は，夫よりも自分の子供を好む。子供は自分のものであることがより確かだからだ。

11. 自然には何の無駄もない。

12. 働く喜びによって，仕事が完璧なものになる。

13. 革命は，些細なことではないが，些細なことから起こる。

14. 恥は，若者にとっては名誉であり，老人にとっては屈辱である。

15. 芸術が目指すのは，これを示すことだ。それは，ものの外見ではなく，内にある本質だ。

16. 最大の美徳は，他人に対して最も役に立つことだ。

17. 唯一の安定状態は，次の状態だ。それは，法の下において，全ての人間が平等だという状態だ。

18. 教育の根は苦いが，その果実は甘い。

19. 知る者は行い，理解する者は教える。

20. 時間は，物事を砕く。すべては時間の力の下で成長し，時間の経過とともに忘れ去られる。

21. 我々が知覚していることや考えていることを意識することは，自分自身の存在を意識することだ。

22. 知覚することは，苦しむことだ。

23. 人は物事を繰り返す存在だ。したがって，優秀さとは，行動ではなく，習慣だ。

24. 始めがうまく行けば，半分できたのと同じだ。

25. 友人がいなければ，誰も生きることを選ばないだろう。他のどんなものが手に入ったとしても。

26. 若者はすぐに騙される。すぐに希望を持ちたがるからだ。

27. 楽観主義者は何もないところにも明かりを見出そうとするが，なぜ悲観主義者はいつもその明かりを吹き消そうとするのだろう？

28. 自分自身を征服せよ。世界ではなく。

29. 難問があれば，いくつにも分割せよ。それを解決するのに実行可能で，かつ必要な部分にまで。

30. 疑えば，知が始まる。

31. あらゆるものごとは自明だ。

32. 自分自身の思考を除けば，我々の力には，絶対的に何も存在しない。

33. 何も後悔させるものなどない。決断しなかったこと以外は。

34. 良識は，この世の全ての中で，最も公平に分配されている。

35. 我思う，ゆえに我あり。

36. 真理を探究したければ，人生において一度は，できる限り深く，あらゆる物事を疑ってみる必要がある。

37. 架空の喜びは，時として，本物の悲しみより価値がある。

38. 精神を向上させるためには，学ぶことを減らし，熟考することを増やすべきだ。

39. 優れた知性を持つだけでは十分ではない。重要なことは，それをうまく活用することだ。

40. 完全数は，完全な人間と同様，極めてまれだ。

41. 人間の誤りの主な原因は，次のことに起因する。それは，幼少期に身に付いた偏見だ。

42. 最も優れた心は，最大の悪徳を持つ。最高の美徳だけでなく。

43. 良き書物を読むことは，過去の最も優れた人間の心と会話をかわすのに似ている。

44. 実際に人々が何を考えているのかを理解するには，彼らの行動に注意を払えばよい。彼らの言葉にではなく。

45. 誰かが私を攻撃する時，私は，自分の魂を高いところに持っていく。その攻撃が届かないところまで。

9 哲学者 (2) 解答

1. Happiness depends upon ourselves.

2. Happiness is the meaning and the purpose (**of**)[1] life, the whole aim and end of human existence.

3. (**He**)[2] who is to be a (**good**)[3] ruler must have first been ruled.

4. Hope is (**a**)[4] waking dream.

5. I count him braver who overcomes his desires (**than**)[5] him who conquers his enemies; for the hardest victory (**is**)[6] over self.

6. It is the (**mark**)[7] of an educated mind to be (**able**)[8] to entertain a thought without accepting it.

7. Love is composed (**of**)[9] a single soul inhabiting two bodies.

8. Man is a (**goal**)[10] seeking animal. His life only has meaning if (**he**)[11] is reaching out and striving for his goals.

9. Misfortune shows those (**who**)[12] are not really friends.

10. Mothers are fonder than fathers of their children because (**they**)[13] are more certain they are their own.

11. Nature (**does**)[14] nothing uselessly.

12. Pleasure in the job puts perfection in (**the**)[15] work.

13. Revolutions are not about trifles, but spring from trifles.

14. Shame (**is**)[16] an ornament to the young; a disgrace to (**the**)[17] old.

15. The aim of art (**is**)[18] to represent not the outward appearance of things, but their inward significance.

16. (**The**)[19] greatest virtues are those which are most useful to other persons.

17. The (**only**)[20] stable state is the one in which all men (**are**)[21] equal before the law.

18. The roots of education are bitter, (**but**)[22] the fruit is sweet.

19. Those that know, do. Those (**that**)[23] understand, teach.

20. Time crumbles things; everything grows old under the power of Time (**and**)[24] is forgotten through the lapse of Time.

21. To (**be**)[25] conscious that we are perceiving or thinking is (**to**)[26] be conscious of our own existence.

22. To perceive (**is**)[27] to suffer.

23. We are what we repeatedly (**do**)[28]. Excellence, then, is not an act, (**but**)[29] a habit.

24. Well begun is half done.

25. Without friends (**no**)[30] one would choose to live, though he had all other goods.

26. Youth (**is**)[31] easily deceived because it is quick to hope.

27. An optimist (**may**)[32] see a light where there is none, but (**why**)[33] must the pessimist always run to blow (**it**)[34] out?

28. Conquer yourself rather than the world.

29. Divide each difficulty into (**as**)[35] many parts as is feasible and necessary to resolve (**it**)[36].

30. Doubt is the origin of wisdom.

31. Everything is self-evident.

32. Except our (**own**)[37] thoughts, there is nothing absolutely in our power.

33. For nothing causes regret and remorse except irresolution.

34. (**Good**)[38] sense is of all things in the world (**the**)[39] most equally distributed.

35. I think, therefore I am.

36. If (**you**)[40] would be a real seeker after truth, it is necessary (**that**)[41] at least once in your life (**you**)[42] doubt, as far as possible, all things.

37. Illusory joy (**is**)[43] often worth more than genuine sorrow.

38. In order to improve the (**mind**)[44], we ought less to learn, than to contemplate.

39. (**It**)[45] is not enough to have a (**good**)[46] mind.   The main thing is to (**use**)[47] it well.

40. Perfect numbers like perfect men are (**very**)[48] rare.

41. The chief cause of human errors is to (**be**)[49] found in the prejudices picked up in childhood.

42. The greatest minds (**are**)[50] capable of the greatest vices as well as (**of**)[51] the greatest virtues.

43. The reading of all good books (**is**)[52] like a conversation with the finest minds of (**past**)[53] centuries.

44. To know what people really think, pay regard to (**what**)[54] they do, rather than what they (**say**)[55].

45. Whenever anyone has offended me, I try to raise (**my**)[56] soul so high that the offense cannot reach (**it**)[57].

10 作家 (2)

1-18 Mark Twain/マーク・トゥエイン (1835 年〜1910 年)
19-30 Anne Frank/アンネ・フランク (1929 年〜1945 年)
31-45 Ernest Hemingway/アーネスト・ヘミングウェイ (1899 年〜1961 年)

CD を聞きながら，(　　　　　) の中に，4 文字以下の英単語を入れて下さい。

1. Keep away from people who try (　　　　　)[1] belittle your ambitions.　Small people always do that, but the really great (　　　　　)[2] you feel that you, too, (　　　　　)[3] become great.

2. Kindness is a language which the deaf can (　　　　　)[4] and the blind can see.

3. Let (　　　　　)[5] endeavor so to live that when (　　　　　)[6] come to die even the undertaker (　　　　　)[7] be sorry.

4. Love seems the swiftest, but it (　　　　　)[8] the slowest of all growths.

5. Name the greatest (　　　　　)[9] all inventors.　Accident.

6. The best way to cheer yourself (　　　　　)[10] is to try to cheer somebody else (　　　　　)[11].

7. The human race has one really effective weapon, and that (　　　　　)[12] laughter.

8. The man who doesn't read good books (　　　　　)[13] no advantage over the man who can't (　　　　　)[14] them.

9. The man who is (　　　　　)[15] pessimist before 48 knows too much; if he is (　　　　　)[16] optimist after it he knows too little.

10. The only (　　　　　)[17] to keep your health is to (　　　　　)[18] what you don't want, drink what you don't (　　　　　)[19] and do what you'd rather not.

11. The proper office (　　　　　)[20] a friend is to side with (　　　　　)[21] when you are in the wrong.　Nearly anybody (　　　　　)[22] side with you when you (　　　　　)[23] in the right.

12. The trouble is not (　　　　　)[24] dying for a friend, but in finding a friend worth dying (　　　　　)[25].

13. To play billiards moderately well is the (　　　　　)[26] of a gentleman; to play it (　　　　　)[27] well is the sign of (　　　　　)[28] misspent life.

14. Truth is stranger than fiction, but it (　　　　　)[29] because Fiction is obliged to stick to possibilities; Truth isn't.

15. What gets (　　　　　)[30] into trouble is not what we don't (　　　　　)[31].　It's what we know for sure (　　　　　)[32] just ain't so.

16. When angry, count to four; when (　　　　　)[33] angry, swear.

17. When in doubt, tell the truth.

18. When (　　　　　)[34] friends begin to flatter you on how young you (　　　　　)[35], it's a sure sign you're getting old.

19. Whoever is happy (　　　　　)[36] make others happy too.

20. A good hearty laugh would help (　　　　　)[37] than ten Valerian pills.

21. As long as this exists, (　　　　　)[38] sunshine and this cloudless sky, and as (　　　　　)[39] as I can enjoy it, how (　　　　　)[40] I be sad?

22. The only (　　　　　)[41] to truly know a person is to argue (　　　　　)[42] them. For when they argue in (　　　　　)[43] swing, then they reveal their true character.

79

10 作家 (2)

23. We all (   )[44] with the objective of being happy, our lives are

    (   )[45] different and yet the same.

24. No one (   )[46] ever become poor by giving.

25. Laziness may appear attractive, but (   )[47] gives satisfaction.

26. Parents can only give good advice or (   )[48] them on the right paths, but

    the final forming (   )[49] a person's character lies in their own hands.

27. Look (   )[50] how a single candle can both defy (   )[51] define

    the darkness.

28. Where there's hope, there's life. It fills us (   )[52] fresh courage and

    makes us strong again.

29. I want to (   )[53] on living even after my death.

30. Everyone has inside of (   )[54] a piece of good news. The

    (   )[55] news is that you don't know (   )[56] great you can

    be! How much (   )[57] can love! What you can accomplish!

    (   )[58] what your potential is!

31. As you (   )[59] older, it is harder to have heroes, but (   )[60] is

    sort of necessary.

32. Every day is (   )[61] new day.

33. Happiness in intelligent people is the rarest thing (   )[62] know.

34. I like to listen. I (   )[63] learned a great deal from listening carefully.

    Most people never listen.

35. In order (   )[64] write about life, first you must live it!

36. (   )^{65} is not made for defeat.   A (   )^{66} can be destroyed but not defeated.

37. My (   )^{67} is to put down on paper (   )^{68} I see and what I (   )^{69} in the best and simplest way.

38. Never think (   )^{70} war, no matter how necessary, nor how justified, (   )^{71} not a crime.

39. The best way (   )^{72} find out if you can trust somebody (   )^{73} to trust them.

40. The writer's job is (   )^{74} to judge, but to seek to understand.

41. There (   )^{75} no friend as loyal as a book.

42. (   )^{76} be a successful father there's one absolute rule: when you (   )^{77} a kid, don't look at it (   )^{78} the first two years.

43. Wars are caused by undefended wealth.

44. What (   )^{79} moral is what you feel good after (   )^{80} what is immoral is what you (   )^{81} bad after.

45. You can't get away from yourself (   )^{82} moving from one place to another.

81

10 作家 (2) 日本語訳

問題英文の日本語訳を確認しよう。

1. こんな人間には近づくな。あなたの夢を萎えさせるような人間に。小さな人間は，いつも，そうする。偉大な人間は，あなたにも成功できると思わせてくれる。

2. 親切とは，こんな言葉だ。耳が聞こえない者も聞くことができ，目が見えない者も見ることができる言葉だ。

3. 一生懸命生きよう。死ぬ時に，葬儀屋も悲しんでくれるほどに。

4. 愛は最も速く育つもののように見えるが，全ての中で，最も育つのが遅いものだ。

5. 最も偉大な発明家の名を挙げよ。それは「偶然」だ。

6. 自分を元気づける最良の方法は，誰か他の人を元気づけてあげることだ。

7. 人類は，極めて効果的な武器を一つ持っている。それは笑いだ。

8. 良書を読まない者は，良書が読めない者となんら変わらない。

9. 48歳より前に悲観主義者になっている者は，物事を知りすぎ，48歳を越えても楽観主義者である者は，物事を知らなさすぎる。

10. 健康を保つ唯一の方法は，食べたくないものを食べ，飲みたくないものを飲み，したくないことをすることだ。

11. 正しい友人は，あなたが間違っている時にあなたの味方をしてくれる。ほとんど誰もが，あなたの味方をしてくれる。あなたが正しい時には。

12. 難しいのは友のために死ぬことではない。命をかける価値がある友を見つけることだ。

13. ビリヤードが，ある程度上手にできるのは，紳士のしるしだ。上手すぎるのは，時間の使い方を間違えた人生のしるしだ。

14. 真実は小説より奇なり。フィクションは可能性を持っていなければならないが，真実はそうではないから。

15. 厄介なのは，何も知らないことではない。実際はそうではないのに，知っていると思い込んでいることだ。

16. むっとしたら，4つまで数えろ。完全に頭に来たら，ののしれ。

17. 迷っている時は，真実を話すことだ。

18. 友人が，若く見えると誉めだしたら，あなたが年をとったというしるしだ。

19. 幸せな人は誰も，他の人をも幸せにする。

20. 心から笑った方がずっと効果がある。薬を10錠飲むより。

21. 太陽の光と雲ひとつない空があり，それを眺めていられる限り，どうして悲しくなれるだろう?

22. 本当に他人の人柄が分かるのは，その人と大喧嘩した時だ。その時こそ，その人の真の人格が

現れる。

23. 私達は皆，幸せになることを目的に生きている。私たちの人生は一人ひとり違うが，結局，皆同じだ。

24. こんな人はいまだかつて一人もいない。与えることで貧しくなった人だ。

25. 怠慢は魅力的に見えるが，働けば，満足感が得られる。

26. 親は子供に助言し，正しい方向に導くことはできるが，最終的な人格形成は子ども自身の手にある。

27. 見てください。たった一本のロウソクが，いかに暗闇を否定し，暗闇を定義することができるかを。

28. 希望があるところに人生がある。希望があれば，新しい勇気が得られ，再び強い気持ちになれる。

29. 私は，死んだ後でも，生き続けたい。

30. 誰もが心に一かけらのいい知らせをもっている。いい知らせとは，まだこのことに気づいていないということだ。自分がどんなに素晴らしい存在になるのか，どれほど深く愛せるのか，何を成し遂げるのか，自分の可能性とは何かということに。

31. 年を重ねると，自分にとってのヒーローを見つけるのが難しくなる。しかし，年を重ねた時こそ，必要だ。

32. やってくる毎日が新しい日だ。

33. 幸福は，知的な人々の中に，ほぼ見出せない。

34. 私は話を聞くのが好きだ。注意深く聞くことで，多くを学んできた。しかし，ほとんどの者は，聞こうとしない。

35. 人生について書きたいなら，まずは，生きなくてはならない。

36. 人間は，負けるように造られてはいない。破壊されることはあっても，負けることはない。

37. 私の目的は，見たことや感じたことを最もうまく単純に書くことだ。

38. 次のように決して考えてはいけない。いかに必要だろうと，いかに正当化できようとも，戦争は，犯罪ではないなどと。

39. 誰かを信頼できるかを試すのに最良の方法は，彼らを信頼してみることだ。

40. 作家の仕事とは，判断を下すことではない。理解しようとすることだ。

41. これほど信頼できる友はいない。書籍ほど。

42. 良き父親になるには，絶対的な規則が一つある。子供を持った時，最初の2年は見ないことだ。

43. 戦争は，これによって引き起こされる。それは，守られていない富だ。

44. 善とは，後味の良いことだ。悪とは，後味の悪いことだ。

45. あなたは，自分からは逃れられない。あちこち旅をしてまわっても。

10 作家（2）解答

1. Keep away from people who try (**to**)[1] belittle your ambitions.　Small people always do that, but the really great (**make**)[2] you feel that you, too, (**can**)[3] become great.

2. Kindness is a language which the deaf can (**hear**)[4] and the blind can see.

3. Let (**us**)[5] endeavor so to live that when (**we**)[6] come to die even the undertaker (**will**)[7] be sorry.

4. Love seems the swiftest, but it (**is**)[8] the slowest of all growths.

5. Name the greatest (**of**)[9] all inventors.　Accident.

6. The best way to cheer yourself (**up**)[10] is to try to cheer somebody else (**up**)[11].

7. The human race has one really effective weapon, and that (**is**)[12] laughter.

8. The man who doesn't read good books (**has**)[13] no advantage over the man who can't (**read**)[14] them.

9. The man who is (**a**)[15] pessimist before 48 knows too much; if he is (**an**)[16] optimist after it he knows too little.

10. The only (**way**)[17] to keep your health is to (**eat**)[18] what you don't want, drink what you don't (**like**)[19] and do what you'd rather not.

11. The proper office (**of**)[20] a friend is to side with (**you**)[21] when you are in the wrong.　Nearly anybody (**will**)[22] side with you when you (**are**)[23] in the right.

12. The trouble is not (**in**)[24] dying for a friend, but in finding a friend worth dying (**for**)[25].

13. To play billiards moderately well is the (**sign**)[26] of a gentleman; to play it (**too**)[27] well is the sign of (**a**)[28] misspent life.

14. Truth is stranger than fiction, but it (**is**)[29] because Fiction is obliged to stick to possibilities; Truth isn't.

15. What gets (**us**)[30] into trouble is not what we don't (**know**)[31].　It's what we know for sure (**that**)[32] just ain't so.

16. When angry, count to four; when (**very**)[33] angry, swear.

17. When in doubt, tell the truth.

18. When (**your**)[34] friends begin to flatter you on how young you (**look**)[35], it's a sure sign you're getting old.

19. Whoever is happy (**will**)[36] make others happy too.

20. A good hearty laugh would help (**more**)[37] than ten Valerian pills.

21. As long as this exists, (**this**)[38] sunshine and this cloudless sky, and as (**long**)[39] as I can enjoy it, how (**can**)[40] I be sad?

22. The only (**way**)[41] to truly know a person is to argue (**with**)[42] them.   For when they argue in (**full**)[43] swing, then they reveal their true character.

23. We all (**live**)[44] with the objective of being happy, our lives are (**all**)[45] different and yet the same.

24. No one (**has**)[46] ever become poor by giving.

25. Laziness may appear attractive, but (**work**)[47] gives satisfaction.

26. Parents can only give good advice or (**put**)[48] them on the right paths, but the final forming (**of**)[49] a person's character lies in their own hands.

27. Look (**at**)[50] how a single candle can both defy (**and**)[51] define the darkness.

28. Where there's hope, there's life.   It fills us (**with**)[52] fresh courage and makes us strong again.

29. I want to (**go**)[53] on living even after my death.

30. Everyone has inside of (**him**)[54] a piece of good news.   The (**good**)[55] news is that you don't know (**how**)[56] great you can be!   How much (**you**)[57] can love!   What you can accomplish!   (**And**)[58] what your potential is!

31. As you (**get**)[59] older, it is harder to have heroes, but (**it**)[60] is sort of necessary.

32. Every day is (**a**)[61] new day.

33. Happiness in intelligent people is the rarest thing (**I**)[62] know.

34. I like to listen.   I (**have**)[63] learned a great deal from listening carefully.   Most people never listen.

35. In order (**to**)[64] write about life, first you must live it!

36. (**Man**)[65] is not made for defeat.   A (**man**)[66] can be destroyed but not defeated.

37. My (**aim**)[67] is to put down on paper (**what**)[68] I see and what I (**feel**)[69] in the best and simplest way.

38. Never think (**that**)[70] war, no matter how necessary, nor how justified, (**is**)[71] not a crime.

39. The best way (**to**)[72] find out if you can trust somebody (**is**)[73] to trust them.

40. The writer's job is (**not**)[74] to judge, but to seek to understand.

41. There (**is**)[75] no friend as loyal as a book.

42. (**To**)[76] be a successful father there's one absolute rule: when you (**have**)[77] a kid, don't look at it (**for**)[78] the first two years.

43. Wars are caused by undefended wealth.

44. What (**is**)[79] moral is what you feel good after (**and**)[80] what is immoral is what you (**feel**)[81] bad after.

45. You can't get away from yourself (**by**)[82] moving from one place to another.

11 芸術家 (2)

1-12 Wolfgang Amadeus Mozart/ヴォルフガング・アマデウス・モーツァルト (1756 年〜1791 年)
13-25 Ludwig van Beethoven/ルートヴィヒ・ヴァン・ベートーヴェン (1770 年〜1827 年)
26-45 Auguste Rodin/オーギュスト・ロダン (1840 年〜1917 年)

CD を聞きながら, (　　　　　　　) の中に, 4 文字以下の英単語を入れて下さい。

1. I am one of those who will (　　　　　)[1] on doing till all doings are at (　　　　　)[2] end.

2. I pay no attention whatever to anybody's praise (　　　　　)[3] blame.　I simply follow my own feelings.

3. I thank my God (　　　　　)[4] graciously granting me the opportunity of learning that death is (　　　　　)[5] key which unlocks the door to our (　　　　　)[6] happiness.

4. Just as people behave to me, so (　　　　　)[7] I behave to them.　When I (　　　　　)[8] that a person despises me and treats me (　　　　　)[9] contempt, I can be as proud as (　　　　　)[10] peacock.

5. Music is my life and my (　　　　　)[11] is music.　Anyone who does not understand this (　　　　　)[12] not worthy of god.

6. Music should never be painful to the (　　　　　)[13] but should flatter and charm it, and thereby always remain music.

7. Neither a lofty degree (　　　　　)[14] intelligence nor imagination nor both together go to (　　　　　)[15] making of genius.　Love, love, love, that (　　　　　)[16] the soul of genius.

8. One must not (　　　　　)[17] oneself cheap here—that is a cardinal point—or (　　　　　)[18] one is done.　Whoever is most impertinent has (　　　　　)[19] best chance.

9. Our riches, being in our brains.

10. The shorter (   )^{20} to do many things is to (   )^{21} only one thing at a time.

11. To (   )^{22} well and eloquently is a very (   )^{23} art, but that an equally great one is (   )^{24} know the right moment to stop.

12. When (   )^{25} am traveling in a carriage, or walking after a (   )^{26} meal, or during the night when I cannot sleep; (   )^{27} is on such occasions that ideas flow (   )^{28} and most abundantly.

13. Artists who have won (   )^{29} are embarrassed by it; thus their first works (   )^{30} often their best.

14. I will seize Fate by the throat. (   )^{31} will not wholly conquer me! Oh, how beautiful it (   )^{32} to live—and live a thousand times (   )^{33}!

15. I wish you music to help (   )^{34} the burdens of life, and to (   )^{35} you release your happiness to others.

16. Music is the mediator between (   )^{36} spiritual and the sensual life.

17. Music is the (   )^{37} which inspires one to new generative processes, and I am Bacchus (   )^{38} presses out this glorious wine for mankind and makes (   )^{39} spiritually drunken.

18. Music should strike fire from the heart of man, (   )^{40} bring tears from the eyes of woman.

19. Nothing is (   )^{41} intolerable than to have to admit to yourself (   )^{42} own errors.

20. Only the pure in heart (   )^{43} make a good soup.

21. The barriers ( )⁴⁴ not erected which can say to aspiring talents and industry, "( )⁴⁵ far and no farther."

22. This is ( )⁴⁶ mark of a really admirable man: steadfastness in ( )⁴⁷ face of trouble.

23. We mortals with immortal minds are ( )⁴⁸ born for sufferings and joys, and one could almost ( )⁴⁹ that the most excellent receive joy through sufferings.

24. You'll give happiness ( )⁵⁰ joy to many other people.   There is nothing better or greater ( )⁵¹ that!

25. Your love makes me at ( )⁵² the happiest and the unhappiest of men.

26. ( )⁵³ is the pleasure of a spirit that enters nature ( )⁵⁴ discovers that it too has a ( )⁵⁵.

27. I am like a moon ( )⁵⁶ shines on an immense, unknown sea where ships never pass.

28. I choose ( )⁵⁷ block of marble and chop off whatever I don't ( )⁵⁸.

29. I invent nothing, I rediscover.

30. In art, immorality cannot exist.   Art ( )⁵⁹ always sacred.

31. Inside you there's an artist you don't know about. He's not interested ( )⁶⁰ how things look different in moonlight.

32. Love your calling ( )⁶¹ passion, it is the meaning of your ( )⁶².

33. Nobody does good to men with impunity.

34. Nothing (   )^{63} a waste of time if you (   )^{64} the experience wisely.

35. Patience is also a form (   )^{65} action.

36. Sculpture is the art of the (   )^{66} and the lump.

37. The artist enriches the (   )^{67} of humanity. The artist delights people with a thousand different shades of feeling.

38. (   )^{68} artist is the confidant of nature, flowers carry on dialogues with (   )^{69} through the graceful bending of their stems and the harmoniously tinted nuances of their blossoms. Every flower (   )^{70} a cordial word which nature directs towards him.

39. The human body (   )^{71} first and foremost a mirror to the soul (   )^{72} its greatest beauty comes from that.

40. The main thing (   )^{73} to be moved, to love, to (   )^{74}, to tremble, to live. Be a (   )^{75} before being an artist.

41. The more simple we are, (   )^{76} more complete we become.

42. The only principle in (   )^{77} is to copy what you (   )^{78}.

43. The work of art is already within (   )^{79} block of marble. I just chop off whatever isn't needed.

44. (   )^{80} the artist there is never anything ugly in nature.

45. True artists (   )^{81} almost the only men who do their (   )^{82} for pleasure.

11 芸術家（2）日本語訳

問題英文の日本語訳を確認しよう。

1. 私は，こんな人間の一人だ。何事も最後までやり遂げる。

2. 他人の賞賛や非難など一切気にしない。自分自身の感性に従うだけだ。

3. 神に感謝する。このことを学ぶ機会を与えてくださったことに対して。死が真の幸福への扉を開ける鍵であることを。

4. 相手の振る舞いに合わせ，私も振る舞う。私を見下し，小ばかにする人がいれば，私は，クジャクのように誇り高く振る舞う。

5. 音楽は自らの人生であり，人生は音楽である。これが理解できない人は，神に値しない。

6. 音楽は決して耳ざわりであってはならない。耳を満足させ，楽しませ，それによって，常に「音楽」でなくてはならない。

7. 高尚な知性や想像力，あるいはその両方があっても天才の形成には至らない。愛，愛，愛，それが，天才の神髄だ。

8. 自分の値打ちを下げてはいけない。それが重要な点だ。そうでなければ，君は終わりだ。最も生意気な人間なら誰でも，絶好のチャンスがある。

9. 我々の財産は，頭の中にある。

10. 多くをなす近道は，一度に一つのことだけをすることだ。

11. 良く喋り，能弁であることは，偉大な技術であるが，それと同様に偉大な技術であるのは，喋るのを止める適切な時を知っていることだ。

12. 馬車で旅をしている時，食後の散歩中，あるいは眠れない夜に，そんな時に，アイデアが最も豊富に湧き出てくる。

13. 芸術家は，名声を勝ちとると，そのことによって苦しむ。したがって，処女作がよく最高傑作となる。

14. 私は，運命の喉もとを締め上げてやる。私は，決して運命に征服されない。どんなに素敵だろう。この人生を千回も生きたなら。

15. 音楽によって，人生の重荷が振り払われ，あなたが他の人々と幸せを分かち合えるように。

16. 音楽は，仲人だ。精神と感覚の世界を結ぶ。

17. 音楽は，ワインで，人に新しいものを作り出させる。私は，バッカスで，人間のためにこの素晴らしいワインを搾り出し，人間を精神的に酔わせる。

18. 音楽は，男の心から炎を打ち出し，女の目から涙を引き出すものであるべきだ。

19. これほど耐えがたいものはない。自分の誤りを認めなければならないことほど。

20. 純粋な心によってのみ，美味しいスープができる。

21. こんな柵は，大志ある才能と勤勉さの前には立てられない。「ここより先は進入禁止」

22. これが真に賞賛すべき人物の証拠だ。苦難に直面し，動揺しないことが。

23. 不死の心を持つ我々は，苦悩と歓喜のためだけに生まれる。その中で最も優れた者が，苦悩を突き抜け，歓喜を勝ち取ると言える。

24. あなたは，多くの人々に幸せや喜びを与える。これほど，崇高で素晴らしいものはない。

25. 君の愛によって，私は，最も幸せな男になるのと同時に，最も不幸な男にもなる。

26. 芸術とは，精神の喜びだ。自然に足を踏み入れ，自然にも魂があることを発見する喜びだ。

27. 私はこんな月に似ている。船が通過することもない広大な未知の海を照らす月だ。

28. 私は大理石の塊を選び，何でも切り落とす。必要としないものは。

29. 私は何も発明しない。ただ再発見するだけだ。

30. 芸術において不道徳は存在しない。芸術は常に神聖だ。

31. あなたの中に，あなたが知らない芸術家がいる。その芸術家は，月光の下で物事がどのように違って見えるかには，興味がない。

32. あなたの使命を愛せ。情熱を持って。それが人生の意味だ。

33. 人に善をなして，咎められないことはない。

34. 何事も時間の無駄ではない。経験を賢く生かすならば。

35. 忍耐もまた行動の一つの形態だ。

36. 彫刻は，穴と塊りの芸術だ。

37. 芸術家は人間の心を豊かにする。芸術家は何千もの異なる感性を持つ人々を楽しませる。

38. 芸術家は自然の親友で，花は芸術家と対話する。茎の優美な曲線と花びらの調和のとれた色合いで。どの花にも，言葉がある。自然が芸術家に心から語りかける言葉だ。

39. 人間の身体は，まず第一にその魂を映し出す鏡であり，そのことによって，人間の最高の美しさが生み出される。

40. 大切なのは，感動すること，愛すること，希望を持つこと，打ち震えること，生きることだ。そして，芸術家である以前に，人間であれ。

41. シンプルになればなるほど，私たちはより完全になる。

42. 芸術の唯一の原則は，見たものを正確に模倣することだ。

43. 芸術作品はすでに大理石の塊の中にある。私はただ切り落とすだけだ。必要のないものを。

44. 芸術家にとって，醜いものは何もない。自然の中には。

45. 真の芸術家とは，唯一の人間だ。喜びのために仕事をする。

11 芸術家 (2) 解答

1. I am one of those who will (**go**)[1] on doing till all doings are at (**an**)[2] end.

2. I pay no attention whatever to anybody's praise (**or**)[3] blame.　I simply follow my own feelings.

3. I thank my God (**for**)[4] graciously granting me the opportunity of learning that death is (**the**)[5] key which unlocks the door to our (**true**)[6] happiness.

4. Just as people behave to me, so (**do**)[7] I behave to them.　When I (**see**)[8] that a person despises me and treats me (**with**)[9] contempt, I can be as proud as (**any**)[10] peacock.

5. Music is my life and my (**life**)[11] is music.　Anyone who does not understand this (**is**)[12] not worthy of god.

6. Music should never be painful to the (**ear**)[13] but should flatter and charm it, and thereby always remain music.

7. Neither a lofty degree (**of**)[14] intelligence nor imagination nor both together go to (**the**)[15] making of genius.　Love, love, love, that (**is**)[16] the soul of genius.

8. One must not (**make**)[17] oneself cheap here—that is a cardinal point—or (**else**)[18] one is done. Whoever is most impertinent has (**the**)[19] best chance.

9. Our riches, being in our brains.

10. The shorter (**way**)[20] to do many things is to (**do**)[21] only one thing at a time.

11. To (**talk**)[22] well and eloquently is a very (**great**)[23] art, but that an equally great one is (**to**)[24] know the right moment to stop.

12. When (**I**)[25] am traveling in a carriage, or walking after a (**good**)[26] meal, or during the night when I cannot sleep; (**it**)[27] is on such occasions that ideas flow (**best**)[28] and most abundantly.

13. Artists who have won (**fame**)[29] are embarrassed by it; thus their first works (**are**)[30] often their best.

14. I will seize Fate by the throat.　(**It**)[31] will not wholly conquer me!　Oh, how beautiful it (**is**)[32] to live—and live a thousand times (**over**)[33]!

15. I wish you music to help (**with**)[34] the burdens of life, and to (**help**)[35] you release your happiness to others.

16. Music is the mediator between (**the**)[36] spiritual and the sensual life.

17. Music is the (**wine**)[37] which inspires one to new generative processes, and I am Bacchus (**who**)[38] presses out this glorious wine for mankind and makes (**them**)[39] spiritually drunken.

18. Music should strike fire from the heart of man, (**and**)[40] bring tears from the eyes of woman.

19. Nothing is (**more**)[41] intolerable than to have to admit to yourself (**your**)[42] own errors.

20. Only the pure in heart (**can**)[43] make a good soup.

21. The barriers (**are**)[44] not erected which can say to aspiring talents and industry, "(**Thus**)[45] far and no farther."

22. This is (**the**)[46] mark of a really admirable man: steadfastness in (**the**)[47] face of trouble.

23. We mortals with immortal minds are (**only**)[48] born for sufferings and joys, and one could almost (**say**)[49] that the most excellent receive joy through sufferings.

24. You'll give happiness (**and**)[50] joy to many other people.   There is nothing better or greater (**than**)[51] that!

25. Your love makes me at (**once**)[52] the happiest and the unhappiest of men.

26. (**Art**)[53] is the pleasure of a spirit that enters nature (**and**)[54] discovers that it too has a (**soul**)[55].

27. I am like a moon (**that**)[56] shines on an immense, unknown sea where ships never pass.

28. I choose (**a**)[57] block of marble and chop off whatever I don't (**need**)[58].

29. I invent nothing, I rediscover.

30. In art, immorality cannot exist.   Art (**is**)[59] always sacred.

31. Inside you there's an artist you don't know about.   He's not interested (**in**)[60] how things look different in moonlight.

32. Love your calling (**with**)[61] passion, it is the meaning of your (**life**)[62].

33. Nobody does good to men with impunity.

34. Nothing (**is**)[63] a waste of time if you (**use**)[64] the experience wisely.

35. Patience is also a form (**of**)[65] action.

36. Sculpture is the art of the (**hole**)[66] and the lump.

37. The artist enriches the (**soul**)[67] of humanity.   The artist delights people with a thousand different shades of feeling.

38. (**The**)[68] artist is the confidant of nature, flowers carry on dialogues with (**him**)[69] through the graceful bending of their stems and the harmoniously tinted nuances of their blossoms.   Every flower (**has**)[70] a cordial word which nature directs towards him.

39. The human body (**is**)[71] first and foremost a mirror to the soul (**and**)[72] its greatest beauty comes from that.

40. The main thing (**is**)[73] to be moved, to love, to (**hope**)[74], to tremble, to live.   Be a (**man**)[75] before being an artist.

41. The more simple we are, (**the**)[76] more complete we become.

42. The only principle in (**art**)[77] is to copy what you (**see**)[78].

43. The work of art is already within (**the**)[79] block of marble.   I just chop off whatever isn't needed.

44. (**To**)[80] the artist there is never anything ugly in nature.

45. True artists (**are**)[81] almost the only men who do their (**work**)[82] for pleasure.

12　実業家（2）

1-2 Thomas Edison/トーマス・エジソン（1847 年～1931 年）
3-23 Andrew Carnegie/アンドリュー・カーネギー（1835 年～1919 年）
24-45 Dale Carnegie/デール・カーネギー（1888 年～1955 年）

CD を聞きながら，（　　　　　　　　）の中に，4 文字以下の英単語を入れて下さい。

1. To invent, you need a good imagination (　　　　　　)[1] a pile of junk.

2. We don't (　　　　　)[2] a millionth of one percent about anything.

3. All honor's wounds are self-inflicted.

4. (　　　　　　)[3] I grow older, I pay less attention (　　　　　)[4] what men say.　I just watch (　　　　　)[5] they do.

5. Children of honest poverty have the (　　　　　)[6] precious of all advantages over those of wealth.

6. Concentration is (　　　　　　)[7] motto—first honesty, then industry, then concentration.

7. Do your duty (　　　　　)[8] a little more and the future will (　　　　　)[9] care of itself.

8. He that cannot reason is (　　　　　)[10] fool.　He that will not (　　　　　)[11] a bigot.　He that dare not (　　　　　)[12] a slave.

9. If you want to (　　　　　)[13] happy, set a goal that commands your thoughts, liberates (　　　　　)[14] energy, and inspires your hopes.

10. It marks a big (　　　　　)[15] in your development when you come (　　　　　)[16] realize that other people can help you do (　　　　　)[17] better job than you could do alone.

11. Mr. Morgan buys (　　　　　)[18] partners; I grow my own.

12. No (　　　　　)[19] becomes rich unless he enriches others.

13. No man will ( )^{20} a great leader who wants to do ( )^{21} all himself or get all the credit ( )^{22} doing it.

14. People who are unable to motivate themselves must ( )^{23} content with mediocrity, no matter how impressive their other talents.

15. The first man ( )^{24} the oyster, the second man gets the shell.

16. ( )^{25} man who dies rich dies disgraced.

17. ( )^{26} men who have succeeded are men ( )^{27} have chosen one line and stuck to it.

18. ( )^{28} secret of success lies not in doing your ( )^{29} work, but in recognizing the right man ( )^{30} do it.

19. The way to become ( )^{31} is to put all your ( )^{32} in one basket and then watch that basket.

20. There is little success where there ( )^{33} little laughter.

21. There is no class so pitiably wretched as that which possesses money ( )^{34} nothing else.

22. There is no use whatever trying to ( )^{35} people who do not help themselves. You cannot ( )^{36} anyone up a ladder unless he be willing to climb himself.

23. ( )^{37} fate hands us a lemon, let's try to ( )^{38} lemonade.

24. A talk is a voyage with ( )^{39} purpose, and it must be charted. The ( )^{40} who starts out going nowhere generally gets there.

12 実業家 (2)

25. All of (   )^{41} tend to put off living.　We (   )^{42} all dreaming of

some magical rose garden over (   )^{43} horizon—instead of enjoying the

roses that are blooming outside our windows today.

26. (   )^{44} fool can criticize, condemn and complain—and most fools

(   )^{45}.

27. Develop success from failures.　Discouragement and failure are two of the sur-

est stepping stones (   )^{46} success.

28. Do the hard jobs first.　The (   )^{47} jobs will take care of themselves.

29. Feeling sorry (   )^{48} yourself, and your present condition, is not only

(   )^{49} waste of energy but the worst habit you could possibly have.

30. Flaming enthusiasm, backed (   )^{50} by horse sense and persistence, is

the quality that (   )^{51} frequently makes for success.

31. Inaction breeds doubt and fear.　Action breeds confidence and courage.　If

(   )^{52} want to conquer fear, do not (   )^{53} home and think

about it.　Go out (   )^{54} get busy.

32. Instead of worrying about what people say (   )^{55} you, why not spend

time trying to accomplish something (   )^{56} will admire.

33. It is the way (   )^{57} react to circumstances that determines our feelings.

34. It isn't what (   )^{58} have, or who you are, (   )^{59} where you are,

or what you (   )^{60} doing that makes you happy or unhappy.　It is

(   )^{61} you think about.

35. Let's not imitate others.　Let's find ourselves and be ourselves.

36. (   )^{62} of the important things in the world have (   )^{63} accomplished by people who have kept on trying (   )^{64} there seemed to be no hope at (   )^{65}.

37. People rarely succeed unless they have fun in what (   )^{66} are doing.

38. Personally I am very fond (   )^{67} strawberries and cream, but I have found that (   )^{68} some strange reason, fish prefer worms. So when I (   )^{69} fishing, I didn't think about what I wanted. I thought (   )^{70} what they wanted.

39. Remember, today is the tomorrow you worried about yesterday.

40. (   )^{71} a chance! All life is a chance. (   )^{72} man who goes the farthest is generally (   )^{73} one who is willing to do and (   )^{74}.

41. The essence of all art is (   )^{75} have pleasure in giving pleasure.

42. The ideas I stand for (   )^{76} not mine. I borrowed them from Socrates. (   )^{77} swiped them from Chesterfield. I stole them from Jesus. (   )^{78} I put them in a (   )^{79}. If you don't like their rules whose would you use?

43. (   )^{80} only way to get the (   )^{81} of an argument is to avoid it.

44. (   )^{82} successful man will profit from his mistakes and (   )^{83} again in a different way.

45. When dealing with people, (   )^{84} us remember we are not dealing with creatures (   )^{85} logic. We are dealing with creatures of emotion, creatures bustling with prejudices (   )^{86} motivated by pride and vanity.

12 実業家 (2) 日本語訳

問題英文の日本語訳を確認しよう。

1. 発明のために必要なのは，優れた想像力とがらくたの山だ。

2. 我々は，何事についても1パーセントの100万分の1も知らない。

3. 自分の名誉の傷は，すべて，自分で傷つけたものだ。

4. 年を重ねるにつれ，人が言うことには以前ほど注意を払わない。ただ，人の行動をじっと見ている。

5. 清く貧しい家庭に育った子供は，かけがえのない宝物が与えられている。裕福な家庭に育った子供とは違って。

6. 集中力は私のモットーだ。一番に誠実さ，次に勤勉さ，そして集中力だ。

7. やるべきことに加えて，もうちょっとだけ行え。そうすれば，未来は自然に開ける。

8. 論じる能力がない者は愚か者だ。論じる気がない者は偏屈者だ。論じる勇気がない者は奴隷だ。

9. 幸せになりたければ，自分の思考を支配する目標を設定し，自分のエネルギーを解放し，希望を抱け。

10. 人間は，こう悟った時に，偉大なる成長を遂げる。他人の助けを借りれば，より優れた仕事ができる，自分一人でやるよりもと悟った時に。

11. モルガン氏はパートナーを買い，私は育てる。

12. 誰も豊かにはなれない。他人を豊かにできなければ。

13. 誰も，偉大なリーダーにはなれない。すべてを自分でやりたがり，すべてを自分の手柄にしたがるような人は。

14. やる気が持てない人は，平凡な人生で満足しなければならない。どんなに素晴らしい才能を持っていても。

15. 最初に来た者が牡蠣を手にし，2番目に来た者が手にするのは，その殻だ。

16. 人が金持ちのままで死ねば，それは，不名誉なことだ。

17. 成功した者は，一つの道を選び，それにしがみついていた者だ。

18. 成功の秘訣は，自分で仕事をすることにはなく，その仕事をする適材を見極めることにある。

19. 富を得る方法は，すべての卵を一つの籠に入れ，見守ることだ。

20. 成功などない。笑い声のないところには。

21. これほど哀れで不幸なものはない。金しか持たない階級ほど。

22. こんなことは，しても無駄だ。それは，自らを助けない者を救うことだ。他人が押し上げることなどできない。梯子を上る意思がない者は。

23. 運命がレモンをくれるなら，それでレモネードを作ってみよう。

24. 話は目的のある航海であり，海図がなければならない。目的を持たずに出発すれば，大抵どこにもたどり着けない。

25. 私たちは，生きることを先延ばしにしている。私たちは皆，水平線の向こうにある魔法のバラ

の庭を夢見ている。今日，窓の外に咲いているバラを楽しむ代わりに。

26. どんな愚者でも批判し，非難し，文句を言うことができる。そして，ほとんどの愚者がそうする。

27. 失敗から成功を生み出せ。挫折と失敗は，間違いなく，成功への足がかりの内の二つだ。

28. 難しい仕事から始めよ。簡単な仕事は自然に終わる。

29. 自分自身と自分の現状を哀れに思うことは，単にエネルギーの無駄遣いであるだけでなく，人間が持ちうる最悪の習慣だ。

30. 燃えるような熱意は，常識と粘り強さに支えられていれば，こんな資質だと言える。最も頻繁に成功を生み出す資質だと。

31. 動かないでいると，疑いと恐れが出てくる。行動すれば，自信と勇気が生み出される。恐れを克服したいと思うのなら，家の中で座って考えたりするな。外に出て，忙しくせよ。

32. 他人にどう思われているかなどと心配する代わりに，こんなことに時間を使ったらどうか。人々が称賛するだろうことを成し遂げることに。

33. 状況に対してどう反応するかによって，私たちの感情が決まる。

34. あなたが何を持っているか，あなたが誰か，あなたが何処にいるか，あるいは，あなたが何をしているかで，あなたが幸福かどうかが決まるわけではない。あなたが何を考えるかで決まるのだ。

35. 人のまねをするな。自分を発見し，自分のままでいろ。

36. この世で重要な物事のほとんどは，こんな者たちによって成し遂げられてきた。全く希望がなさそうに見えても挑戦し続けてきた者たちにだ。

37. 人は，めったに成功しない。自分がしていることが楽しくなければ。

38. 私はイチゴの練乳掛けが大好きだが，魚はミミズが大好きだ。だから魚釣りに行く時は，自分の好物は考えず，魚の好物を考える。

39. 次のことを心に留めておけ。今日は，明日だ。昨日あなたが心配していた日だ。

40. チャンスを生かせ！全人生はチャンスだ。成功する人は，一般的に，チャンスを生かそうとする人だ。

41. すべての芸術の本質は，喜びを感じることだ。喜びを与える事に。

42. 私が掲げるアイデアは私のものではない。私はソクラテスから借用し，チェスターフィールドからくすね，キリストから盗んだ。それを本にも書いた。彼らの規則が気に入らなければ，誰のアイデアを使えばいいのか？

43. 議論から最大の利益を得る唯一の方法は，議論を避けることだ。

44. 成功する人は，自分の失敗から学び，別の方法でやり直す。

45. 人を扱う場合には，次のことを覚えておこう。論理的生物を扱っているのではない。扱っているのは感情的生物で，偏見に満ち，自尊心と虚栄心によって行動するということを。

12 実業家 (2) 解答

1. To invent, you need a good imagination (**and**)[1] a pile of junk.

2. We don't (**know**)[2] a millionth of one percent about anything.

3. All honor's wounds are self-inflicted.

4. (**As**)[3] I grow older, I pay less attention (**to**)[4] what men say.   I just watch (**what**)[5] they do.

5. Children of honest poverty have the (**most**)[6] precious of all advantages over those of wealth.

6. Concentration is (**my**)[7] motto—first honesty, then industry, then concentration.

7. Do your duty (**and**)[8] a little more and the future will (**take**)[9] care of itself.

8. He that cannot reason is (**a**)[10] fool.   He that will not (**is**)[11] a bigot.   He that dare not (**is**)[12] a slave.

9. If you want to (**be**)[13] happy, set a goal that commands your thoughts, liberates (**your**)[14] energy, and inspires your hopes.

10. It marks a big (**step**)[15] in your development when you come (**to**)[16] realize that other people can help you do (**a**)[17] better job than you could do alone.

11. Mr. Morgan buys (**his**)[18] partners; I grow my own.

12. No (**man**)[19] becomes rich unless he enriches others.

13. No man will (**make**)[20] a great leader who wants to do (**it**)[21] all himself or get all the credit (**for**)[22] doing it.

14. People who are unable to motivate themselves must (**be**)[23] content with mediocrity, no matter how impressive their other talents.

15. The first man (**gets**)[24] the oyster, the second man gets the shell.

16. (**The**)[25] man who dies rich dies disgraced.

17. (**The**)[26] men who have succeeded are men (**who**)[27] have chosen one line and stuck to it.

18. (**The**)[28] secret of success lies not in doing your (**own**)[29] work, but in recognizing the right man (**to**)[30] do it.

19. The way to become (**rich**)[31] is to put all your (**eggs**)[32] in one basket and then watch that basket.

20. There is little success where there (**is**)[33] little laughter.

21. There is no class so pitiably wretched as that which possesses money (**and**)[34] nothing else.

22. There is no use whatever trying to (**help**)[35] people who do not help themselves.   You cannot (**push**)[36] anyone up a ladder unless he be willing to climb himself.

23. (**When**)[37] fate hands us a lemon, let's try to (**make**)[38] lemonade.

24. A talk is a voyage with (**a**)[39] purpose, and it must be charted.   The (**man**)[40] who starts out going nowhere generally gets there.

25. All of (**us**)[41] tend to put off living.   We (**are**)[42] all dreaming of some magical rose garden over (**the**)[43] horizon—instead of enjoying the roses that are blooming outside our windows today.

26. (**Any**)⁴⁴ fool can criticize, condemn and complain—and most fools (**do**)⁴⁵.

27. Develop success from failures. Discouragement and failure are two of the surest stepping stones (**to**)⁴⁶ success.

28. Do the hard jobs first. The (**easy**)⁴⁷ jobs will take care of themselves.

29. Feeling sorry (**for**)⁴⁸ yourself, and your present condition, is not only (**a**)⁴⁹ waste of energy but the worst habit you could possibly have.

30. Flaming enthusiasm, backed (**up**)⁵⁰ by horse sense and persistence, is the quality that (**most**)⁵¹ frequently makes for success.

31. Inaction breeds doubt and fear. Action breeds confidence and courage. If (**you**)⁵² want to conquer fear, do not (**sit**)⁵³ home and think about it. Go out (**and**)⁵⁴ get busy.

32. Instead of worrying about what people say (**of**)⁵⁵ you, why not spend time trying to accomplish something (**they**)⁵⁶ will admire.

33. It is the way (**we**)⁵⁷ react to circumstances that determines our feelings.

34. It isn't what (**you**)⁵⁸ have, or who you are, (**or**)⁵⁹ where you are, or what you (**are**)⁶⁰ doing that makes you happy or unhappy. It is (**what**)⁶¹ you think about.

35. Let's not imitate others. Let's find ourselves and be ourselves.

36. (**Most**)⁶² of the important things in the world have (**been**)⁶³ accomplished by people who have kept on trying (**when**)⁶⁴ there seemed to be no hope at (**all**)⁶⁵.

37. People rarely succeed unless they have fun in what (**they**)⁶⁶ are doing.

38. Personally I am very fond (**of**)⁶⁷ strawberries and cream, but I have found that (**for**)⁶⁸ some strange reason, fish prefer worms. So when I (**went**)⁶⁹ fishing, I didn't think about what I wanted. I thought (**about**)⁷⁰ what they wanted.

39. Remember, today is the tomorrow you worried about yesterday.

40. (**Take**)⁷¹ a chance! All life is a chance. (**The**)⁷² man who goes the farthest is generally (**the**)⁷³ one who is willing to do and (**dare**)⁷⁴.

41. The essence of all art is (**to**)⁷⁵ have pleasure in giving pleasure.

42. The ideas I stand for (**are**)⁷⁶ not mine. I borrowed them from Socrates. (**I**)⁷⁷ swiped them from Chesterfield. I stole them from Jesus. (**And**)⁷⁸ I put them in a (**book**)⁷⁹. If you don't like their rules whose would you use?

43. (**The**)⁸⁰ only way to get the (**best**)⁸¹ of an argument is to avoid it.

44. (**The**)⁸² successful man will profit from his mistakes and (**try**)⁸³ again in a different way.

45. When dealing with people, (**let**)⁸⁴ us remember we are not dealing with creatures (**of**)⁸⁵ logic. We are dealing with creatures of emotion, creatures bustling with prejudices (**and**)⁸⁶ motivated by pride and vanity.

13 政治家 (2)

1–5 Benjamin Franklin/ベンジャミン・フランクリン (1706 年〜1790 年)
6–22 Napoléon Bonaparte/ナポレオン・ボナパルト (1769 年〜1821 年)
23–45 John F. Kennedy/ジョン・F・ケネディ (1917 年〜1963 年)

CD を聞きながら，（　　　　　　　）の中に，4 文字以下の英単語を入れて下さい。

1. There never was a good war or (　　　　　　)[1] bad peace.

2. Tolerate no uncleanliness in body, clothes, or habitation.

3. (　　　　　　)[2] no hurtful deceit; think innocently and justly, and, if you speak,

    speak accordingly.

4. Watch (　　　　　)[3] little things; a small leak will sink a great (　　　　　)[4].

5. Whatever is begun in anger ends in shame.

6. A leader (　　　　　)[5] a dealer in hope.

7. A throne is (　　　　　)[6] a bench covered with velvet.

8. Ability is nothing without opportunity.

9. Courage is like (　　　　　)[7]; it must have hope for nourishment.

10. Death (　　　　　)[8] nothing, but to live defeated and inglorious is

    (　　　　　)[9] die daily.

11. Four hostile newspapers are more to be feared (　　　　　)[10] a thousand bayo-

    nets.

12. Imagination rules the world.

13. It requires more courage to suffer (　　　　　)[11] to die.

14. Never interrupt your enemy when he (　　　　　)[12] making a mistake.

15. Religion is what keeps the poor (　　　　　)[13] murdering the rich.

16. Take time to deliberate, (　　　　　)^{14} when the time for action comes, stop

thinking (　　　　) ^{15} go in.

17. The best way (　　　　) ^{16} keep one's word is not to (　　　　) ^{17} it.

18. The human race is governed by its imagination.

19. (　　　　) ^{18} most dangerous moment comes with victory.

20. The word *impossible* is (　　　　) ^{19} in my dictionary.

21. There are but two powers in (　　　　) ^{20} world, the sword and the mind. In

(　　　　) ^{21} long run the sword is always beaten by (　　　　) ^{22} mind.

22. Victory belongs to the most persevering.

23. A (　　　　) ^{23} may die, nations may rise and (　　　　) ^{24}, but an idea lives

on.

24. All (　　　　) ^{25} us do not have equal talents, but (　　　　) ^{26} of us should

have an equal opportunity to develop (　　　　) ^{27} talents.

25. Ask not what your country can (　　　　) ^{28} for you; ask what you

(　　　　) ^{29} do for your country.

26. Change is the (　　　　) ^{30} of life. And those who look (　　　　) ^{31} to the

past or the present (　　　　) ^{32} certain to miss the future.

27. Confident and unafraid, we (　　　　) ^{33} labor on—not toward a strategy of

annihilation but toward (　　　　) ^{34} strategy of peace.

28. Do not pray for (　　　　) ^{35} lives. Pray to be stronger men.

103

13 政治家（2）

29. Efforts and courage (   )^{36} not enough without purpose and direction.

30. Forgive your enemies, but never forget their names.

31. If (   )^{37} free society cannot help the many who (   )^{38} poor, it cannot save the few (   )^{39} are rich.

32. Let us never negotiate out (   )^{40} fear. But let us never fear (   )^{41} negotiate.

33. Liberty without learning is always in peril; learning without liberty is always in vain.

34. Mankind (   )^{42} put an end to war, (   )^{43} war will put an end (   )^{44} mankind.

35. Only those who dare to fail greatly (   )^{45} ever achieve greatly.

36. Our most basic common link is (   )^{46} we all inhabit this planet. We all breathe (   )^{47} same air. We all cherish our children's future.

37. (   )^{48} problems are man-made; therefore, they can be solved by (   )^{49}. Man's reason and spirit have often solved the seemingly unsolvable. I believe they (   )^{50} do it again.

38. The greater our knowledge increases, the greater (   )^{51} ignorance unfolds.

39. The ignorance of one voter in a democracy impairs the security (   )^{52} all.

40. The time to repair the (   )^{53} is when the sun is shining.

41. There (   )^{54} risks and costs to a program of action, but (   )^{55} are far less than the long-range risks (   )^{56} costs of comfortable inaction.

42. Those who make peaceful revolution impossible will make violent revolution inevitable.

43. (   )^{57} must use time as a (   )^{58}, not as a crutch.

44. We need (   )^{59} who can dream of things that never (   )^{60}.

45. When written in Chinese, the word *crisis* is composed (   )^{61} two characters. One represents danger and the other represents opportunity.

13 政治家 (2) 日本語訳

問題英文の日本語訳を確認しよう。

1. 良い戦争や悪い平和などない。

2. 黙認してはいけない。身体，衣服，住居が不潔であることを。

3. 害があるような嘘をつくな。悪意を持たず，公正に考え，そして話すなら，それに応じて話せ。

4. 小さなことでも見落とすな。ほんの少しの水漏れから，大きな船も沈む。

5. 何でも，怒りから始まったものは，恥に終わる。

6. リーダーとは，希望を配る人だ。

7. 玉座は，ベンチに過ぎない。ビロードで覆われたベンチだ。

8. 能力も機会が与えられなければ，価値がない。

9. 勇気は愛に似ている。育てるには，希望が要る。

10. 死ぬことは何でもないが，打ち負かされて，名誉を失ったまま生きるのは，毎日死ぬのと同じだ。

11. 敵意ある四つの新聞は，千の銃剣より恐ろしい。

12. 想像力が，世界を支配する。

13. 苦しむ方が勇気を必要とする。死ぬよりも。

14. 敵を邪魔するな。やつらが間違いを犯している間は。

15. 宗教とは，このようなものだ。それによって，貧しい者が金持ちを殺すことを思い留まるような。

16. じっくり考えろ。しかし，行動する時が来たら，考えるのをやめて，進め。

17. 約束を守る最良の方法は，決して約束しないことだ。

18. 人間は，支配されている。その想像力によって。

19. 最大の危険な瞬間は，勝利の瞬間にやってくる。

20. 私の辞書には，「不可能」という文字はない。

21. 世界には二つの力しかない。剣と精神だ。最終的には，剣は，必ず精神に打ち負かされる。

22. 勝利は，最も忍耐強い人にやってくる。

23. 人は死に，国は興亡するかもしれないが，思想は生き続ける。

24. 我々すべてが，同等の才能を持っているわけではない。しかし，我々は皆，才能を伸ばすための同等の機会を持つべきだ。

25. 国があなたのために何をしてくれるかを問うのではなく，あなたが国のために何ができるかを問え。

26. 変化とは人生の法則である。人が，過去と現在しか見なければ，確実に未来を見失う。

27. 自信を持って恐れず，私たちは働き続けなければならない。人類絶滅の戦略に向かってではなく，平和の戦略に向かって。

28. 楽な人生を願い求めるな。より強い人間になれるよう願え。

29. 努力と勇気は十分ではない。目的と方針がなければ。

30. あなたの敵を許せ。しかし，やつらの名前は決して忘れるな。

31. 自由社会が，貧しい多数の人々を助けられなければ，富める少数の人々も守れないだろう。

32. 恐怖から交渉をしないようにしよう。しかし同時に，交渉を恐れないようにもしよう。

33. 自由は，学問を伴わなければ，常に危険であり，学問は，自由を伴わなければ，常に空虚である。

34. 人類は戦争に終止符を打たなければならない。そうでなければ，戦争が人類に終止符を打つことになる。

35. 大きな失敗を恐れない者のみが，偉大なことを成し遂げる。

36. 我々の最も基本的なつながりは，誰もがこの小さな惑星に住んでいるということだ。誰もが同じ空気を吸っている。誰もが子供たちの未来を大事に思っている。

37. 私たちの問題は，人間が作り出したものだ。したがって，人間が解決できる。これまで，人間の理知と精神は，解決不可能だと思われることもしばしば解決してきた。これからも，またそうできると私は信じている。

38. 知識が増すほど，我々の無知が明らかになる。

39. 有権者が一人でも民主主義に対して無知であると，全有権者の安全が低下してしまう。

40. 屋根を修理するなら，日が照っている時だ。

41. 行動には，常に危険や代償が伴う。しかしそれは，取るに足りないことだ。行動をせずに生じる長期的な危険やコストと較べれば。

42. 平和的革命ができない者は，どうしても，暴力的革命を行ってしまう。

43. 我々は，時を道具として使わなければならない。よりかかる松葉杖としてではなく。

44. 我々は，こんな人物を必要としている。今までになかったものを夢見ることができる人物だ。

45. 中国語で書くと，「危機」という言葉は二つの漢字でできている。一つは危険を表し，もう一つは好機を表している。

13 政治家 (2) 解答

1. There never was a good war or (**a**)^1 bad peace.

2. Tolerate no uncleanliness in body, clothes, or habitation.

3. (**Use**)^2 no hurtful deceit; think innocently and justly, and, if you speak, speak accordingly.

4. Watch (**the**)^3 little things; a small leak will sink a great (**ship**)^4.

5. Whatever is begun in anger ends in shame.

6. A leader (**is**)^5 a dealer in hope.

7. A throne is (**only**)^6 a bench covered with velvet.

8. Ability is nothing without opportunity.

9. Courage is like (**love**)^7; it must have hope for nourishment.

10. Death (**is**)^8 nothing, but to live defeated and inglorious is (**to**)^9 die daily.

11. Four hostile newspapers are more to be feared (**than**)^{10} a thousand bayonets.

12. Imagination rules the world.

13. It requires more courage to suffer (**than**)^{11} to die.

14. Never interrupt your enemy when he (**is**)^{12} making a mistake.

15. Religion is what keeps the poor (**from**)^{13} murdering the rich.

16. Take time to deliberate, (**but**)^{14} when the time for action comes, stop thinking (**and**)^{15} go in.

17. The best way (**to**)^{16} keep one's word is not to (**give**)^{17} it.

18. The human race is governed by its imagination.

19. (**The**)^{18} most dangerous moment comes with victory.

20. The word *impossible* is (**not**)^{19} in my dictionary.

21. There are but two powers in (**the**)^{20} world, the sword and the mind.   In (**the**)^{21} long run the sword is always beaten by (**the**)^{22} mind.

22. Victory belongs to the most persevering.

23. A (**man**)^{23} may die, nations may rise and (**fall**)^{24}, but an idea lives on.

24. All (**of**)^{25} us do not have equal talents, but (**all**)^{26} of us should have an equal opportunity to develop (**our**)^{27} talents.

25. Ask not what your country can (**do**)^{28} for you; ask what you (**can**)^{29} do for your country.

26. Change is the (**law**)^{30} of life.   And those who look (**only**)^{31} to the past or the present (**are**)^{32} certain to miss the future.

27. Confident and unafraid, we (**must**)^{33} labor on—not toward a strategy of annihilation but toward (**a**)^{34} strategy of peace.

28. Do not pray for (**easy**)[35] lives.　Pray to be stronger men.

29. Efforts and courage (**are**)[36] not enough without purpose and direction.

30. Forgive your enemies, but never forget their names.

31. If (**a**)[37] free society cannot help the many who (**are**)[38] poor, it cannot save the few (**who**)[39] are rich.

32. Let us never negotiate out (**of**)[40] fear.　But let us never fear (**to**)[41] negotiate.

33. Liberty without learning is always in peril; learning without liberty is always in vain.

34. Mankind (**must**)[42] put an end to war, (**or**)[43] war will put an end (**to**)[44] mankind.

35. Only those who dare to fail greatly (**can**)[45] ever achieve greatly.

36. Our most basic common link is (**that**)[46] we all inhabit this planet.　We all breathe (**the**)[47] same air.　We all cherish our children's future.

37. (**Our**)[48] problems are man-made; therefore, they can be solved by (**man**)[49].　Man's reason and spirit have often solved the seemingly unsolvable.　I believe they (**can**)[50] do it again.

38. The greater our knowledge increases, the greater (**our**)[51] ignorance unfolds.

39. The ignorance of one voter in a democracy impairs the security (**of**)[52] all.

40. The time to repair the (**roof**)[53] is when the sun is shining.

41. There (**are**)[54] risks and costs to a program of action, but (**they**)[55] are far less than the long-range risks (**and**)[56] costs of comfortable inaction.

42. Those who make peaceful revolution impossible will make violent revolution inevitable.

43. (**We**)[57] must use time as a (**tool**)[58], not as a crutch.

44. We need (**men**)[59] who can dream of things that never (**were**)[60].

45. When written in Chinese, the word *crisis* is composed (**of**)[61] two characters.　One represents danger and the other represents opportunity.

14 教育家・活動家 **(2)**

1-3 Helen Keller/ヘレン・ケラー（1880 年～1968 年）
4-12 Malcolm X/マルコム X（1925 年～1965 年）
13-45 Martin Luther King, Jr./マーティン・ルーサー・キング・ジュニア（1929 年～1968 年）

CD を聞きながら，（　　　　　　　　）の中に，4 文字以下の英単語を入れて下さい。

1. Life is an exciting business and most exciting （　　　　　　）[1] it is lived for others.

2. Although the world is （　　　　　　）[2] of suffering, it is full also （　　　　　　）[3] the overcoming of it.

3. I thank God for （　　　　　　）[4] handicaps. For through them, I have found myself, my （　　　　　　）[5] and my God.

4. If you don't stand for something, （　　　　　　）[6] will fall for anything.

5. If you （　　　　　　）[7] no critics, you'll likely have no success.

6. My alma mater was books, （　　　　　　）[8] good library. I could spend the rest of （　　　　　　）[9] life reading.

7. Education is our passport to the future, （　　　　　　）[10] tomorrow belongs to the people who prepare for it today.

8. （　　　　　　）[11] he is motivated no one can change more completely （　　　　　　）[12] the man who has been （　　　　　　）[13] the bottom.

9. To have once been （　　　　　　）[14] criminal is no disgrace. To remain a criminal is （　　　　　　）[15] disgrace.

10. People don't realize how a man's whole life can be changed （　　　　　　）[16] one book.

11. If you're not ready to die （　　　　　　）[17] it, take the word 'freedom' out （　　　　　　）[18] your vocabulary.

12. It's time for us to submerge （　　　　　　）[19] differences and realize that it is best （　　　　　　）[20] us to first see that we （　　　　　　）[21] the same problem, a common problem.

13. A genuine leader is (　　　　　　)^{22} a searcher for consensus but a molder of consensus.

14. (　　　　　　)^{23} lie cannot live.

15. All progress is precarious, and (　　　　　　)^{24} solution of one problem brings us face to face (　　　　　　)^{25} another problem.

16. Almost always, the creative dedicated minority has made the world better.

17. An individual (　　　　　　)^{26} not started living until he can rise above the narrow confines (　　　　　　)^{27} his individualistic concerns to the broader concerns of all humanity.

18. Darkness cannot drive (　　　　　　)^{28} darkness; only light can do that. Hate cannot drive (　　　　　　)^{29} hate; only love can do (　　　　　　)^{30}.

19. Every man must decide whether he will walk (　　　　　　)^{31} the light of creative altruism or in the darkness (　　　　　　)^{32} destructive selfishness.

20. Freedom is never voluntarily given by the oppressor; it must (　　　　　　)^{33} demanded by the oppressed.

21. I have a dream (　　　　　　)^{34} my four little children will one day live in (　　　　　　)^{35} nation where they will not be judged by (　　　　　　)^{36} color of their skin but by the content (　　　　　　)^{37} their character.

22. I have a dream that one day (　　　　　　)^{38} the state of Mississippi, a state sweltering with (　　　　　　)^{39} heat of injustice, sweltering with the heat (　　　　　　)^{40} oppression, will be transformed into an oasis of freedom (　　　　　　)^{41} justice.

23. I have a dream that one day every valley shall (　　　　　　)^{42} exalted, and every hill and mountain shall be made (　　　　　　)^{43}, the rough places will be made plain, and (　　　　　　)^{44} crooked places will be made straight, and the glory (　　　　　　)^{45} the Lord shall be revealed and all flesh shall see (　　　　　　)^{46}

together.

24. I have a dream that one day (   )[47] the red hills of Georgia, the sons (   )[48] former slaves and the sons of former slave owners will (   )[49] able to sit down together at (   )[50] table of brotherhood.

25. I have a dream that one (   )[51] this nation will rise up and (   )[52] out the true meaning of its creed: "(   )[53] hold these truths to be self-evident, that all (   )[54] are created equal."

26. I have a dream that one (   )[55], down in Alabama, with its vicious racists, with (   )[56] governor having his lips dripping with the words of "interposition" (   )[57] "nullification"—one day right there in Alabama little black boys and black girls will (   )[58] able to join hands with little white boys (   )[59] white girls as sisters and brothers.

27. In the (   )[60], we will remember not the words of (   )[61] enemies, but the silence of our friends.

28. Injustice anywhere is (   )[62] threat to justice everywhere.

29. Life's most persistent and urgent question is: What (   )[63] you doing for others?

30. Love is the (   )[64] force capable of transforming an enemy into a friend.

31. Nothing in (   )[65] the world is more dangerous than sincere ignorance and conscientious stupidity.

32. (   )[66] lives begin to end the day we decide (   )[67] become silent about things that matter.

33. Our scientific power has outrun our spiritual power. We (   )[68] guided missiles and misguided men.

34. Take the first step (   )[69] faith. You don't have to see the whole stair-case, (   )[70] take the first step.

35. The old (   )⁷¹ of an eye for an (   )⁷² leaves everyone blind.

36. The ultimate measure of a man is (   )⁷³ where he stands in moments of comfort and convenience, but where (   )⁷⁴ stands at times of challenge and controversy.

37. The ultimate tragedy is (   )⁷⁵ the oppression and cruelty by the bad people (   )⁷⁶ the silence over that by the (   )⁷⁷ people.

38. Those who are not looking for happiness are (   )⁷⁸ most likely to find it, because those who (   )⁷⁹ searching forget that the surest way to be happy is to seek happiness for others.

39. True peace is (   )⁸⁰ merely the absence of tension: it is the presence (   )⁸¹ justice.

40. We must accept finite disappointment, but never lose infinite hope.

41. (   )⁸² must combine the toughness of the serpent with (   )⁸³ softness of the dove, a tough mind (   )⁸⁴ a tender heart.

42. We must develop and maintain the capacity (   )⁸⁵ forgive. He who is devoid of the power (   )⁸⁶ forgive is devoid of the power to love. There (   )⁸⁷ some good in the worst of (   )⁸⁸ and some evil in the (   )⁸⁹ of us. When we discover this, (   )⁹⁰ are less prone to hate our enemies.

43. (   )⁹¹ must learn to live together as brothers or perish together (   )⁹² fools.

44. When you are right, you cannot be (   )⁹³ radical; when you are wrong, you cannot be (   )⁹⁴ conservative.

45. You are not only responsible for (   )⁹⁵ you say, but also for (   )⁹⁶ you do not say.

14 教育家・活動家 (2) 日本語訳

問題英文の日本語訳を確認しよう。

1. 人生は胸躍るものだ。そして最も胸が躍るのは，人のために生きる時だ。

2. 世の中はつらいことで満ち溢れているが，それを克服することでも満ち溢れている。

3. 私は，自分のハンディキャップに対して，神に感謝している。このハンディキャップを通して，私は，自分自身，生涯の仕事，そして神を見つけることができたからだ。

4. あなたが何かのために闘わなければ，どんなことに対しても，失敗する。

5. あなたを批判する人がいなければ，あなたは，おそらく，成功しない。

6. 私の母校は，書物，つまり，良き図書館だ。残りの生涯をすべて読書に費やしてもいい。

7. 教育こそが未来へのパスポートだ。明日という日は，今日，明日の準備をする人たちのものだ。

8. いったん動機づけられると，これほど見違えるように変わる人間はいない。人生のどん底にいた人間ほど。

9. ひとたび犯罪を犯したとしても，それは恥ではない。犯罪を犯し続けるならば，それは，恥だ。

10. 誰もこのことを理解していない。いかに人の一生が，丸ごと変わってしまうかということを。たった一冊の本によって。

11. 自由のために死ぬ準備がないなら，「自由」という言葉をあなたの辞書から消せ。

12. 今こそ，その時だ。我々が，違いにこだわらず，同じ，共通の問題を持っていることに着目することが，最良であると認識する時だ。

13. 真のリーダーとは，合意を探す者ではなく，合意を形成する者だ。

14. 嘘は，生き続けられない。

15. すべての進歩は不安定で，一つの問題を解決しても，我々はまた他の問題に直面する。

16. ほとんどいつも，創造的でひたむきな少数派によって，世界がより良くなってきた。

17. 人は，初めて本当の人生を歩み始める。個人的な狭い関心事を越え，人類全体に関わる広い関心事に向かうようになって初めて。

18. 闇は，闇によって追い払えない。光だけがそうすることができる。憎しみは，憎しみによって追い払えない。愛だけがそうすることができる。

19. 人は誰でも，決断しなければならない。創造的な利他主義の光の道を歩むか，破壊的な利己主義の闇の道を歩むかを。

20. 自由は，決して圧制者の側が自発的に与えない。自由は，抑制されている者が要求しなくてはならない。

21. 私には夢がある。いつの日か，国民が立ち上がり，この国の信条の真の意味の下で生きるという夢だ。「我々は，自明の真理とみなす。すべての人間は平等に造られいることを」という信条だ。

22. 私には夢がある。いつの日か，あらゆる谷が高められ，あらゆる丘と山は低められ，でこぼこした所は平らにされ，曲がった道はまっすぐにされ，そして，神の栄光が啓示され，生きとし生けるものがそれを共に見るという夢だ。

23. 私には夢がある。いつの日か，ジョージア州の赤土の丘の上で，かつての奴隷の息子たちとか

つての奴隷所有者の息子たちが，兄弟というテーブルに一緒に座ることができるという夢だ。

24. 私には夢がある。いつの日か，私の4人の幼な子が，肌の色によってではなく，人格によって評価される国に住むという夢だ。

25. 私には夢がある。いつの日か，ミシシッピ州さえ，不正と抑圧の炎熱でうだるほどの州さえ，自由と正義のオアシスに変わるという夢だ。

26. 私には夢がある。いつの日か，アラバマ州さえ，邪悪な人種差別主義者や，「干渉」や「無効」という言葉ばかり使う州知事がいる，まさにそのアラバマ州でさえ，いつの日か，黒人の少年少女が白人の少年少女と兄弟姉妹として手をつなげるようになるという夢だ。

27. 結局，我々は，覚えているものだ。敵の言葉ではなく，友人の沈黙を。

28. どこにおける不正でも，あらゆるところの公正への脅威となる。

29. 人生において，最も永続的でしかも緊急の問いかけは，次の問いかけだ。「あなたは，今，何をしているのか。他人のために」

30. 愛だけが，唯一の力だ。敵を友人に変えることができる。

31. この世で，これほど危険なものはない。誠実な無知と良心的な愚かさだ。

32. 我々の命は，終わりに向かい始める。問題になっていることに沈黙しようと決めた日に。

33. 科学の力が，精神的な力を超えてきてしまっている。我々は，ミサイルを正しく撃てるようになったが，同時に，人間を誤った方向に導くようにもなってしまった。

34. 信じて，最初の一歩を踏み出せ。階段のすべてが見えなくてもよい。とにかく最初の一歩を踏み出せ。

35. 「目には目を」という古い法を守っていたら，世の中の人々はみな盲目になってしまう。

36. 人の最終的な評価は，これによって決まる。快適で便利に暮らしている時に何をしているかではなく，困難や論争に立ち向かっている時に何をしているかによって。

37. 究極の悲劇は，悪人の圧制や残酷さではなく，善人がそれに対して沈黙していることである。

38. 人は，幸せを探そうとしなければ，最も確実に幸せを見つけることができる。というのも，幸せを探している人は，幸せになる最も確実な方法を忘れているからだ。他人の幸せを探すという。

39. 真の平和とは，単に緊張がないだけではない。そこに正義が存在することだ。

40. 我々は，限りある失望を受け入れなければならない。しかし，無限の希望を失ってはならない。

41. 我々は，ヘビの強靱性とハトの柔軟性を持たなければならない。不屈の精神と優しい心を。

42. 人を許すことを覚え，身につけなければならない。人を許す力量がない者には，人を愛する力もない。最悪の人間にもどこか取り柄があり，最高の人間にも悪い面がある。これが分かれば，敵を憎む気持ちが薄れる。

43. 我々は，兄弟姉妹として，共に生きる術を学ばなければならない。それができなければ，愚か者として共に滅びる。

44. あなたが正しい時，過激になりすぎてはいけない。あなたが間違っている時，保守的になりすぎてはいけない。

45. 人は，次のことに責任を持たなければならない。「発言する」ことだけでなく，「発言しない」ということにも。

14 教育家・活動家 (2) 解答

1. Life is an exciting business and most exciting (**when**)[1] it is lived for others.

2. Although the world is (**full**)[2] of suffering, it is full also (**of**)[3] the overcoming of it.

3. I thank God for (**my**)[4] handicaps. For through them, I have found myself, my (**work**)[5] and my God.

4. If you don't stand for something, (**you**)[6] will fall for anything.

5. If you (**have**)[7] no critics, you'll likely have no success.

6. My alma mater was books, (**a**)[8] good library. I could spend the rest of (**my**)[9] life reading.

7. Education is our passport to the future, (**for**)[10] tomorrow belongs to the people who prepare for it today.

8. (**Once**)[11] he is motivated no one can change more completely (**than**)[12] the man who has been (**at**)[13] the bottom.

9. To have once been (**a**)[14] criminal is no disgrace. To remain a criminal is (**the**)[15] disgrace.

10. People don't realize how a man's whole life can be changed (**by**)[16] one book.

11. If you're not ready to die (**for**)[17] it, take the word 'freedom' out (**of**)[18] your vocabulary.

12. It's time for us to submerge (**our**)[19] differences and realize that it is best (**for**)[20] us to first see that we (**have**)[21] the same problem, a common problem.

13. A genuine leader is (**not**)[22] a searcher for consensus but a molder of consensus.

14. (**A**)[23] lie cannot live.

15. All progress is precarious, and (**the**)[24] solution of one problem brings us face to face (**with**)[25] another problem.

16. Almost always, the creative dedicated minority has made the world better.

17. An individual (**has**)[26] not started living until he can rise above the narrow confines (**of**)[27] his individualistic concerns to the broader concerns of all humanity.

18. Darkness cannot drive (**out**)[28] darkness; only light can do that. Hate cannot drive (**out**)[29] hate; only love can do (**that**)[30].

19. Every man must decide whether he will walk (**in**)[31] the light of creative altruism or in the darkness (**of**)[32] destructive selfishness.

20. Freedom is never voluntarily given by the oppressor; it must (**be**)[33] demanded by the oppressed.

21. I have a dream (**that**)[34] my four little children will one day live in (**a**)[35] nation where they will not be judged by (**the**)[36] color of their skin but by the content (**of**)[37] their character.

22. I have a dream that one day (**even**)[38] the state of Mississippi, a state sweltering with (**the**)[39] heat of injustice, sweltering with the heat (**of**)[40] oppression, will be transformed into an oasis of freedom (**and**)[41] justice.

23. I have a dream that one day every valley shall (**be**)[42] exalted, and every hill and mountain shall be made (**low**)[43], the rough places will be made plain, and (**the**)[44] crooked places will be made straight, and the glory (**of**)[45] the Lord shall be revealed and all flesh shall see (**it**)[46] together.

24. I have a dream that one day (**on**)[47] the red hills of Georgia, the sons (**of**)[48] former slaves and the sons of former slave owners will (**be**)[49] able to sit down together at (**the**)[50] table of brotherhood.

25. I have a dream that one (**day**)[51] this nation will rise up and (**live**)[52] out the true meaning of its creed: "(**We**)[53] hold these truths to be self-evident, that all (**men**)[54] are created equal."

26. I have a dream that one (**day**)[55], down in Alabama, with its vicious racists, with (**its**)[56] governor having his lips dripping with the words of "interposition" (**and**)[57] "nullification"—one day right there in Alabama little black boys and black girls will (**be**)[58] able to join hands with little white boys (**and**)[59] white girls as sisters and brothers.

27. In the (**end**)[60], we will remember not the words of (**our**)[61] enemies, but the silence of our friends.

28. Injustice anywhere is (**a**)[62] threat to justice everywhere.

29. Life's most persistent and urgent question is: What (**are**)[63] you doing for others?

30. Love is the (**only**)[64] force capable of transforming an enemy into a friend.

31. Nothing in (**all**)[65] the world is more dangerous than sincere ignorance and conscientious stupidity.

32. (**Our**)[66] lives begin to end the day we decide (**to**)[67] become silent about things that matter.

33. Our scientific power has outrun our spiritual power. We (**have**)[68] guided missiles and misguided men.

34. Take the first step (**in**)[69] faith. You don't have to see the whole staircase, (**just**)[70] take the first step.

35. The old (**law**)[71] of an eye for an (**eye**)[72] leaves everyone blind.

36. The ultimate measure of a man is (**not**)[73] where he stands in moments of comfort and convenience, but where (**he**)[74] stands at times of challenge and controversy.

37. The ultimate tragedy is (**not**)[75] the oppression and cruelty by the bad people (**but**)[76] the silence over that by the (**good**)[77] people.

38. Those who are not looking for happiness are (**the**)[78] most likely to find it, because those who (**are**)[79] searching forget that the surest way to be happy is to seek happiness for others.

39. True peace is (**not**)[80] merely the absence of tension: it is the presence (**of**)[81] justice.

40. We must accept finite disappointment, but never lose infinite hope.

41. (**We**)[82] must combine the toughness of the serpent with (**the**)[83] softness of the dove, a tough mind (**and**)[84] a tender heart.

42. We must develop and maintain the capacity (**to**)[85] forgive. He who is devoid of the power (**to**)[86] forgive is devoid of the power to love. There (**is**)[87] some good in the worst of (**us**)[88] and some evil in the (**best**)[89] of us. When we discover this, (**we**)[90] are less prone to hate our enemies.

43. (**We**)[91] must learn to live together as brothers or perish together (**as**)[92] fools.

44. When you are right, you cannot be (**too**)[93] radical; when you are wrong, you cannot be (**too**)[94] conservative.

45. You are not only responsible for (**what**)[95] you say, but also for (**what**)[96] you do not say.

参考文献

牧秀樹（2018）『The Minimal English Test（最小英語テスト）研究』開拓社，東京.

癒しツアー（2020）「名言・格言・ことわざ集」https://iyashitour.com/meigen，2020
年5月20日取得.

牧　秀樹（まき　ひでき）

　岐阜大学地域科学部教授。1995 年にコネチカット大学にて博士号（言語学）を取得。研究対象は，言語学と英語教育。

　主な著書・論文：*Essays on Irish Syntax*（Dónall P. Ó Baoill 氏と共著，2011 年，開拓社），*Essays on Mongolian Syntax*（Lina Bao, Megumi Hasebe 氏と共著，2015 年，開拓社），*Essays on Irish Syntax II*（Dónall P. Ó Baoill 氏と共著，2017 年，開拓社），"The Minimal English Test: A New Method to Measure English as a Second Language Proficiency"（Kenichi Goto, Chise Kasai 氏と共著，*Evaluation & Research in Education* 23，2010 年），「The Minimal English Test（最小英語テスト）の有用性」（長谷川信子編『日本の英語教育の今，そして，これから』2013 年，開拓社），『The Minimal English Test（最小英語テスト）研究』（2018 年，開拓社），『誰でも言語学』，『最小英語テスト（MET）ドリル』〈標準レベル：高校生から社会人〉，〈センター試験レベル〉，『中学生版 最小英語テスト（jMET）ドリル』（以上，2019 年，開拓社），「英語 monogrammar シリーズ」『関係詞』『比較』『準動詞』『助動詞・仮定法』『時制・相』（以上，2020 年，監修，開拓社）など。

金言版 最小英語テスト（kMET）ドリル

ISBN978-4-7589-2333-0　C0082

著作者　　牧　秀樹
発行者　　武村哲司
印刷所　　日之出印刷株式会社

2020 年 10 月 25 日　第 1 版第 1 刷発行©

発行所　　株式会社 開拓社

〒113-0023　東京都文京区向丘 1-5-2
電話　（03）5842-8900（代表）
振替　00160-8-39587
http://www.kaitakusha.co.jp